JOSHIN JOSEPH

WORK-LIFE BALANCE: A REVIEW

A critical review of research in the realm of work-life balance

Work-Life Balance: A Review

A critical review of research in the realm of work-life balance

Cover design: Joshin Joseph

Set by: Joshin Joseph

Published by: Joshin Joseph

Type of book: Paperback

ISBN: 978-93-5351-535-5

Contract Information: -

Joshin Joseph

Pariyath H, Kurianad P.O,

Kottayam, Kerala, India – 686663

Email: joshinpariyath@gmail.com

"Miracle means the existing knowledge is unable to explain the event occurred, nothing more nothing less"

ACKNOWLEDGEMENT

I take this opportunity to convey my heartfelt thanks to Dr. Deepu Jose Sebastian, my doctoral research guide for his support and motivation that instil me to come up with this book.

Joshin Joseph

CONTETS

LIST OF TABLES

LIST OF ABBREVIATIONS

Short Form	Expanded Form	Short Form	Expanded Form
AF	Adaptability in family	PSWF	Positive Spill over from Work to Family
AG	Agreeableness	QL	Qualitative
ANOVA	Analysis of Variance	QT	Quantitative
BCE	Before Common Era	REL	Religiosity
BPO	Business Process Outsourcing	SBI	State Bank of India
BSSS	Berlin Scale of Social Support	SD	Standard Deviation
CC	Cognitive Cohesion	SG	Perceived Instrumental Support
CCIL	Clearing Corporation of India Ltd.	SS	Support Seeking Mentality
CFI	Confirmatory Fit Index	SWB	Subjective Well Being
CI	Confidence Interval	SWLB	Satisfaction with Work-life Balance
CIS	Career Identity Silence	TLI	Tucker-Lewis Index
CO	Conscientiousness	TI	Turnover Intension
CRS	Centrality of Religiosity Scale	TIPI	Ten Item Personality Measure
CR	Care Responsibility	WC	Work Commitment
EC	Emotional Cohesion	WFC	Work Family Conflict
ED	Educational Qualification	WFE	Work Family Enrichment
ELoC	External Locus of Control	WIPL	Work Interference with Personal Life
EM	Emotional Stability	WIF	Work Interference with Family
EX	Extraversion	WIFL	Work Interference with Family Life
FLIW	Family Life Interference with Work	WLB	Work Life Balance
FIW	Family Interference with Work	WLIB	Work-Life Imbalance
FS	Family Satisfaction	WLBS	Work Life Balance Strategies
FWC	Family to Work Conflict	WLC	Work Life Conflict
GFI	Goodness of Fit Index	WLS	Work Life Satisfaction
GLM	General Linear Models	WPLE	Work or Personal Life Enrichment
GoI	Government of India	WSF	Work-Schedule Fit
HoW	Hours of Work	WS	Work Shift
ILO	International Labour Organisation	WSs	Work Satisfaction
ILoC	Internal Locus of Control	YE	Year of Experience
INC	Monthly Income	PSWF	Positive Spill over from Work to Family
IOC	Indian Oil Corporation	QL	Qualitative
IT	Information Technology	QT	Quantitative
ITes	Information Technology Enabled Sector	REL	Religiosity
JD	Job Demand	OCF	Open communication in family
JDs	Job Description	OCB	Organisation Citizenship Behaviour
JRI	Job Related Issues	OP	Openness
JS	Job Satisfaction	PLIW	Personal Life Interference with Work
LoC	Locus of Control	PLS	Personal Life Satisfaction
M	Mean	POS	Perceived Organisational Support

PREFACE

This book 'WORK-LIFE BALANCE: A REVIEW' predominantly discuss the headway of work-life balance research. The book is based on my experience as a work-life balance research scholar. Notes and write-ups prepared as part of my doctoral degree were colossal in designing the content of this book. The work-life balance is a concept which is identified as pervasive for every employee irrespective of his/her living environment. However, the concept of work-life balance become prevalent only in the 21st century. The prime objective of the book is to critically examine the research happened in the field of work-life balance research.

In this book rather than drawing a general review based on the collective genesis of the work-life balance research, this book critically examined each work specifically. A book of this kind, which incorporates a tailor-made review and evaluation of the work-life balance studies specifically will be immensely helpful for researchers and academicians who explore work-life balance as they can easily grasp and pinpoint the pitfalls as well as underexplored areas in the field of work-life balance research that needs to be addressed further. No inferences were made out of review rather classifications and categorisations were made objectively on the basis of common theme shared among the studies, in order to facilitate reader extrapolation.

Joshin Joseph

CHAPTER - 1

WORK-LIFE BALANCE - AN INTRODUCTION

"Science is a way of thinking much more than it is a body of knowledge"

-   *Carl Sagan (Astronomer)*

In a work titled 'balancing work life and home life: what can organisations do to help' Hall & Richter (1989) states that proper balancing of the work and family life is essential for the wellbeing of the employee as a whole. The physical resources available in the family and organisational together with the psychological resources processed by the employee themselves are very essential for the work-life balance. Work is the mean to the life and therefore, it's impossible to segregate the work out human's life. Work being the part of life, it should be aligned together with the other life domains for the wellbeing of an employee (Bellman, 1990). The body needs food and shelter to get them requires work (Grazia, 1962). The work is an integral part of the life which is essential for survival. Balancing on work life with personal life is very indispensable for the wellbeing of the employee.

1.1 Work-Life Balance - Etymology

The term 'work-life balance' was first used in the United Kingdom in the late 1970s to describe the balance between an individual's work and personal life. However, work-life programs existed as early as the 1930s. The W.K.Kellogg Company created four six-hour shifts to replace the traditional three daily eight-hour shift, and the new shift resulted in increased employee morale and efficiency. In 1938 the U.S legalised 44-hour work week (U.S Department of Labour Wage and Hour Division, 1938). Europeans (specifically by the 'New Ways to Work and the Working Mothers Association in the United Kingdom) introduced the term work-life balance in the late of 1970s in order to describe the balance between an individual's work and personal life, several studies (Burnett, 2011; Clews & Associates). In the United States, the phrase 'work-life balance' was first used in the year 1986 in the relation of prioritisation of hours between work and non-work activities, several studies (Coradon Health, 2016; Burnett, 2011; Clews & Associates). It is unjust and impossible to tie-up the authorship of the work-life balance concept to a specific person or an event. It's a concept that got evolved gradually around the world at the different epoch in locus with the socio-cultural environment prevailed in that particular habitation.

The public parlance is that the work-life balance research seeds during the mid of 19th century. Clark (2000) defined work-life balance (WLB) as "satisfaction and good functioning at work and at home, with a minimum of role conflict". Work-life-family balance is a self-defined state of wellbeing. It allows one to effectively manage multiple responsibilities at work, home, and in the community; it supports physical, emotional, family and community health (Human Resources and Skills Development Canada HRSDC, 2004). HRSDC recognizes work-life-family balance as the inter-relatedness of work life and life apart from work. Chandrasekar et al., (2013) defined work-life balance as a satisfactory level of involvement or 'fit' between the multiple roles in a person's life. Sheokand and Priyanka (2013) stated that work-life balance is the proper prioritizing between 'work' (career and ambition) on one hand and 'life' (pleasure, leisure, family and spiritual development) on the other. In the referendum to the above-said definitions, it is very evident that work-life balance is an all-inclusive concept that reflects the overall life satisfaction, wellbeing, and domain demand coincidence of the employee. Work-life balance is a lifelong issue with lifelong relevance (Goodwin & Graebe, 2017).

Over the past years there was a change in the terminology from work-family balance to work-life balance, it acknowledges the need to consider the domain besides family and thereby recognises the diversity of the current world, people now a day undertake wide range of activities that are outside the preview of family domain (Stepanova, 2012). Because of the unsystematic methodology followed it's very difficult to draw objective conclusions about the content scope of the work-life balance concept (Albertsen, Rafnsdóttir, Grimsmo, Tómasson, & Kauppinen, 2008). Because of its psycho-social blend, WLB studies often adopt non-experimental and qualitative design. Hence, it becomes very difficult to establish the magnitude and chronology of the relationship between variables. Furthermore, variables in the psycho-social environment often have a bidirectional relationship and the WLB research often failed to inculcate non-recursive models while exploring WLB. Until industrialisation work was commuted at the premise of the worker. The work-home divide is the enunciation of industrialisation. The industrialisation sliced out the work out of the family (Young & Willmott, 1977).

In a work titled 'balancing work life and home life: what can organisations do to help' Hall & Richter, 1989 states that proper balancing of the work and family life is essential for the wellbeing of the employee as a whole. They pointed out that physical resources available both at the family and organisational level as well as psychological resources processed by the employee themselves are very essential for the proper management for work and family life balance. Hall and Richter find that what employees really need is to have clear boundaries and some degree of separation between their work and home lives. They offer guidelines to individuals and organizations on effective management of these boundaries. And also, specify the lack of an organisational model to track this issue. Later in 1990 Geoffrey M in a journal article mentioned that the work is only a part of the life and therefore the work should be balanced with life. In that article, he also specifies the need for having a cap on hours worked and the necessity of leisure and family engagement in the successful management of life (Bellman, 1990).

1.2 The Panoptic Nature of Work-life Balance

Work-life balance is a concept that has an inclination with a cyclical environment around an individual. All the interactive environment around an individual wield sway over his work-life balance level. Socio-cultural environment, work environment, and family environment were the most protuberant forces that shape the work-life balance level of an employee, in unison, it should be noted that the factors that influence work-life balance are permeable and temporal in nature. Because of the permeability and temporal status of work-life balance forces, it's researchers often failed to define the cause of work-life balance with consistency. Furthermore, the magnitude and strength that the environmental factors have on the work-life balance level of an individual depend upon the stock of cognitive resource available with that specific individual/employee.

The relationship between work-life balance and personal psychology has underexplored. Though, fractional the researchers have identified the relationship between work-life balance is personal psychology of the employee. A positive and significant relationship between type A personality and internal locus of control and work-life balance (Ediriweera & Weerakkody, 2010). Woman having personality disorders have a significantly lower level of life balance and quality of life as compare with women without a personality disorder (Larivière, et al., 2016). That is, the psychological resource available with an employee can act as a catalyst that interact with the environmental factors and thereby defines the work-life balance level. Similarly, the social categories and coping resources available with an individual (employee) moderates the relationship between work family interface with work, family and other individual related outcomes. The success of the work-family fit is determined by the successfulness of strategies implemented by an individual at work and family domain. When the strategies become successful it results in role ease and work-family enhancement. Whereas when the strategies become unsuccessful it results in role ease role strain and thereby work-family conflict arises (Voydanoff, 2002).

Individuals, as well as organisations, share the responsibility of maintaining work/life balance of the employees. Although a variety of work/life balance benefits and policies are offered, they are only used by a minority of employees. Employees are unable to make use of work-life balance policies offered by organisations and because of this, the expected impact of work-life balance programmes was often diluted (Bulger & Fisher, 2012). Work-life balance policies (leave, work-hour, recreation, work, work/home, study) failed to enhance the work-life balance level (work-life balance initiatives were unable to increase the level of job satisfaction and organisational commitment. Similarly, such initiatives did not have any impact on work-to-family conflict, family-to-work conflict, job stress and intention to quit) of employees (Branch, 2008).

The aftermath of work-life balance on an individual includes enhanced job satisfaction, improved mental wellbeing, and better physical health. Whereas the consequences of work-life imbalance were poor psychological wellbeing, feituage, poor physical health, increased level of conflict both in the personal as well as in the work life, lack of life satisfaction, lack of family satisfaction, etc., While considering the organisation work-life balance will benefit the organisation by enhancing the productivity, reduced employee turnover, reduced accident and better job satisfaction. Understanding about self is the basic skill that enables one to manage his life (Ingham, 2007; Greenberg & Avigdor, 2009). Psychological factors and capability have relation with work-life balance (Rantanen, Kinnunen, MaunO, & Tillemann, 2010; Carnegie, 1986). Happiness and balance were an inner urge and it should be generated from individuals themselves and the external environment have only a limited scope to play with.

References

Albertsen, K., Rafnsdóttir, G. L., Grimsmo, A., Tómasson, K., & Kauppinen, K. (2008). Workhours and worklife balance. *SJWEH Suppl*, 14-21.

Bellman, G. M. (1990). Balancing Your Work in Your Life. *Training and Development Journal* .

Branch, S. (2008). *The Effects of Organisational Work-Life Balance Initiatives on Accountants in New Zealand* . Canterbury: Sarah Branch.

Bulger, C. A., & Fisher, G. G. (2012). Ethical Imperatives of Work/Life Balance. In N. P. Reilly, M. J. Sirgy, & C. A. Gorman, *Work and Quality of Life* (pp. 181-201). Springer.

Burnett, K. (2011). Chapter 2: People/HR. In K. Burnett, *Practical Contact Center Collaboration* (pp. 20-60). Pittsburgh: Rose Dog Books.

Carnegie, D. (1986). *How to Enjoy Your Life and Your Job.* New York: Pocket Books.

Chandarasekar, K. S., Suma, S., Renjini, S., & Ansu, S. (2013). Study on Work-Life Balance among the executives in IT Industry with special reference to Technopark, Trivandrum, Kerala. *Asian Journal of Multidimensional Research, 2*(3).

Clark, S. C. (2000). Work/Family Border Theory: A New Theory of Work/Family Balance. *Human Relations*, 747-770. doi:10.1177/0018726700536001

Clews, B., & Associates. (n.d.). *Work and Personal Life Balance.* Retrieved from BarbClews: www.barbclews.com

Coradon Health. (2016, March 27). *Health & Wellbeing.* Retrieved from Coradon Health: www.corazonhealth.co.uk

Ediriweera, A., & Weerakkody, W. (2010). The Relationship between Personality and Work Life Balance; An Empirical Study of Bank Executives in Western Province. *Annual Research Symposium* (pp. 80-96). Kelaniya: University of Kelaniya.

Goodwin, G. C., & Graebe, S. F. (2017). Work-Life Balance. In G. C. Goodwin, & S. F. Graebe, *A Doctorate and Beyond* (pp. 179-185). Cham: Springer.

Grazia, S. d. (1962). Toward the Work Society. In S. d. Grazia, *Of Time Work and Leisure* (pp. 35-62). New York: The Twentieth Century Fund.

Greenberg, C. L., & Avigdor, B. S. (2009). *Praise for What Happy Working Mothers Know.* New Jersey: John Wiley & Sons, Inc.

Hall, D. T., & Richter, J. (1989). Balancing Work Life and Home Life: What Can Organizations Do to Help? *The Academy of Management Executive*, 213-223. Retrieved from http://www.jstor.org/stable/4164832

Ingham, G. (2007). *Motivate People Getting the Best from Yourself and Others.* London: Dorling Kindersley Limited .

Larivière, N., Denis, C., Payeur, A., Ferron, A., Levesque, S., & Rivard, G. (2016). Comparison of Objective and Subjective Life Balance Between Women With and Without a Personality Disorder. *Psychiatric Quarterly, 87*(4), 663-673. doi:10.1007/s11126-016-9417-3

Rantanen, J., Kinnunen, U., MaunO, S., & Tillemann, K. (2010). Introducing Theoretical Approaches to Work-Life Balance and Testing a New Typology Among Professionals. In S. Kaiser, M. J. Ringlstetter, D. R. Eikhof, & M. P. Cunha (Eds.), *Creating Balance?* (pp. 27-46). Springer Berlin Heidelberg. doi:10.1007/978-3-642-16199-5

Sheokand, K. S., & Priyanka. (2013). Work Life Balance: An Overview of Indian Companies. *International Journal of Research in Commerce and Management*, 138-143.

Stepanova, O. (2012). *Work-Life Balance in Organizational Subcultures The Case of Mutua.* PhD Thesis, University of Barcelona, Barcelona.

U.S Deartment of Labour Wage and Hour Division. (1938). Hours of Work. *The Fair Labor Standards Act Of 1938.* United States of America: WH Publication.

Voydanoff, P. (2002). Linkages Between the Work-family Interface and Work, Family, and Individual OutcomesAn Integrative Model. *Journal of Family Issues, 23*(1), 138-164.

Weerakkody, W., & Ediriweera, A. (2010). Demographic Balance and Work Life Balance; An Empirical Studyof Bank Executives in Western Province.

Iternational Research Conference on Business and Information (pp. 189-203). Kelaniya: University of Kelaniya.

Young, M., & Willmott, P. (1977). *The Symmetrical Family: A Study of Work and Leisure in the London Region.* London: Penguin Book.

CHAPTER – 2

MEANING AND DEFINITION OF WORK-LIFE BALANCE

"We must always take sides. Neutrality helps the oppressor, never the victim. Silence encourages the tormentor, never the tormented"

- *Elie Wiesel (Writer)*

The term work-life balance was coined as a concept that epitomize the balance between work and personal/non-work life (several studies Smeltzer, et al., 2016; Voydanoff, 2005; Kirchmeyer, Perceptions of Nonwork-to-Work Spillover: Challenging the Common View of Conflict-Ridden Domain Relationships, 1992; Kirchmeyer, Nonwork Participation and Work Attitudes: A Test of Scarcity vs. Expansion Models of Personal Resources, 1992). Although, the research fails to bring conscience among researchers with regard to a theoretical and conceptual definition for work-life balance (several studies, Glasgow & Sang, 2016; Smeltzer, et al., 2016; Brough, et al., 2014; Poulose & N, 2014; Kalliath & Brough, 2008). The multiplicity of the definition often diluted the clarity as well as the scope of the WLB construct. However, the pervasive need of employees to achieve work-life balance has never been questioned. Several studies (e.g., Joseph & Sebastian 2017; Glasgow & Sang, 2016; Greenhaus & Singh, 2004) proved that the work-life balance is a topic commonly applicable to all working individuals irrespective of gender, age, and cultural dimensions.

2.1 The Work-Life Balance Definitions

The following table 2.1 illustrates the list of various definitions for work-life balance proposed by different work-life balance researchers chronologically in the order of descending.

Table 2.1
Work-Life Balance Definitions

Proposer	Definition AND Meaning
(Jindal, 2016)	Work-life balance is the ability of an individual to schedule the hours of professional and personal life in such a way that promote a healthy and peaceful life.
(Kumari & Selvi, 2015)	Work-life balance is defined as the state of equilibrium at which the demand from the personal life and professional life are equal.
(Gananapalli, 2015)	Work-life balance is defined as an enjoyable equilibrium between professional and personal life of a working individual.
(Yadav & Rani, 2015)	Work-life balance is the successful management and organisation between remunerative work and the other roles and the responsibilities that are important to people as 'individualised' human beings and as a part of the society.
(Monica.M, 2015)	Refers to an individual's perception of the degree to which she/he is experiencing positive relationships between work and family roles, where the relationships are viewed as compatible and at equilibrium with each other.
(Morganson, Litano, & O'Neill, 2014)	Work-family balance is the total effect and outcome of work-family enrichment and work-family conflict.

(G.Shiva, 2013)	Defined Work-life balance as those practices employed by individuals in sticking a balance between demands from their work and family lives.
(Rajkumar, 2014)	Work life balance is considered as a state of wellbeing to handle multiple responsibilities in life.
(Bruton, 2012)	It is a situation at which individuals are able to carry out their roles effectively and having time other activities like family and leisure.
(Ervin, 2012)	Work-life balance is a situation at which an employee spends sufficient time not only at work but also at family, with friends and on hobbies.
(Brougha, et al., 2014)	Work–life balance is as an individual's subjective appraisal of the accord between his/her work and non-work activities and life more generally.
(Malaviya, 2012)	Work-life balance is not only the balance towards work and family but also inculcate other life activities.
(Chandarasekar, S, Nair, & S.R, 2013)	Work-life balance is defined as a satisfactory level of involvement or 'fit' between the multiple roles in a person's life.
(Hutcheson, 2012)	Work-life balance is a state at which one have control over this life together with achievement and satisfaction.
(Sree, 2013)	Work-life balance is the summarised effect of satisfaction towards various aspects of work and family conditions.
(Sheokand & Priyanka, 2013)	Work-life balance is defined as the proper prioritizing between 'work' (career and ambition) on one hand and 'life' (pleasure, leisure, family and spiritual development) on the other.
(Swarnalatha, 2013)	Work-life balance is the level of satisfaction that a person has both in his personal life and in work life.
(Viswanathan & Jeyakumaran, 2013)	Work-life balance is defined as the ability of a person to exercise control over work and family roles without compromising in between. Together with fulfilling the needs of society and friends, while performing the family and work role.
(Stepanova, 2012)	Work-life balance is the degree and magnitude of integration between professional and personal life.

(Sunderaraj, 2012)	Work-life balance is the managing as well as juggling act in between paid work and other all activities that a person finds significant to him.
(Ajay KR & Amanjot, 2012)	Work-life balance is a border concept that includes proper prioritizing of work and life activities.
(Parida, 2012)	It is a state at which one person is having the right combination and participation both in paid work and in other aspects of his life in terms of working hours and working conditions.
(Jyothi, 2011)	Work-life balance is a term used to describe those practices at the workplace that acknowledge and aim to support the need of employees in achieving a balance between the demand their family (life) and work life.
(Rantanen, Kinnunen, MaunO, & Tillemann, 2010)	Work-life balance refers to a low level of work to non-work conflict together with a high level of work to non-work enhancement. Whereas satisfactory balance is one attained when both the work to non-work conflict as well as enhancement was almost equal.
(Grzywacz & Dawn S. Carlson, 2007)	Work-family balance is defined as the accomplishment of role-related expectations that are negotiated and shared between an individual and his or her role-related partners in the work and family domains.
(Littig, 2008)	Work-life balance refers to an effectively combining of work life with private obligations or aspirations.
(Kalliath & Brough, 2008)	Work-life balance is the perception of an individual that his work, as well as non-work activities, are compactable and able to promote his growth in accordance with current life.
(Fleetwood, 2006)	Work-life balance is a theme at which employees have control over work and work environment.
(Redmond, Valiulis, & Drew, 2006)	Work-life balance is an effective balance between work and domestic responsibilities.
(State Services Commission, 2005)	Work-life balance is the right combination of participation in paid work (defined by hours and working conditions) and other aspects in their lives.
(Grzywacz & Bass, 2003)	Defines work-life balance as a situation at which when there is a high level of family to work facilitation together with a low level of work to family conflict.

(Frone, Work-family balance, 2003)	Defines work-life balance as a multidimensional construct whose nature (work to family and family to work), as well as an effect (conflict and facilitation), have a bidirectional impact.
(Greenhaus, Collins, & Shaw, The relation between work-life balance and quality of life, 2003)	Defines work-family balance as the extent to which an individual is equally engaged in an equally satisfied with his or her work and family role.
(Greenhaus & Singh, Work and Family, Relationship between, 2004)	The extent to which individuals are equally involved in-and equally satisfied with their work role and their family role.
(Kodz, Harper, & Dench, 2002)	Work-life balance is that situation at which an individual's paid work have a healthy balance with the life outside the work
(Hill, Hawkins, Ferris, & Weitzman, 2001)	Work-family balance may be defined as the degree to which an individual is able to simultaneously balance the temporal, emotional, and behavioral demands of both paid work and family responsibilities.
(Clark, 2000)	Defines work/family balance as satisfaction and good functioning at work and at home with a minimum of role conflict.
(Milkie & Peltola, 1999)	Work-life balance is a subjective feeling of an individual about various different aspects of harmony.

The multiplicity of the work-life balance definition often threatens the content validity of the work-life balance concept. All the above definition of WLB can be summarised under the different head on the basis of the conceptual interweave in its core theme.

2.1.1 Equal role participation hypothesis of work-life balance

According to the equal role participation hypothesis, work-life balance is the outcome of equal involvement, both psychologically as well as physically across multiple roles in life. The important proponents of equal role participation hypothesis were Chandarasekar, 2013; Ajay K.R & Amanjot, 2012; Parida, 2012; State Services Commission, 2005; Greenhaus, Collins, & Shaw, 2003; and Greenhaus & Singh, 2004.

Critique: - The major critique against an equal role participation hypothesis is the practical applicability of the concept. Equal physical involvement across multiple roles can be assured with the help of efficient time management. However, the concept of equitable psychological involvement across multiple roles can only be defined theoretically. That is, the equal role participation hypothesis defines work-life balance as a concept which is practically ill-defined. Similarly, the domain role significance is purely individualistic in nature. For example, in the case of an employee who is predominantly workaholic in nature finds the work enthusiastic and enjoys undertaking the work in comparison with his fellow worker who is not workaholic in nature. Therefore, defining work-life balance as the outcome of equal role participation across multiple roles has severe theoretical as well as operational drawbacks.

2.1.2 Domain satisfaction hypothesis of work-life balance

The domain satisfaction hypothesis states that the work-life balance is the outcome of life domain satisfaction. A life domain is a slice that represents a unique role system. Work, family, religion., each represents a separate domain in life, and the 'life' represents a bunch of domains.

Therefore, an individual is said to have a balanced work-life when he experiences satisfaction across various domains in his/her life. The major proponents of domain satisfaction hypothesis of work-life balance were Hutcheson, 2012; Swarnalatha, 2013; Greenhaus & Singh, Work and Family, Relationship between, 2004; and Greenhaus, Collins, & Shaw, 2003.

Critique: - According to domain satisfaction hypothesis, work-life balance is the outcome of work and life satisfaction. That is the satisfaction at the personal life domain together with satisfaction in the work-life domain results work-life balance. Clarke, Koach, & Hill, (2004) empirically tested the satisfaction hypothesis of work-life balance and found that satisfaction not necessarily to be followed by the experience of work-life balance. Which means, defining work-life balance as the outcome of domain satisfaction lacks empirical validity. Similarly, another critique against satisfaction model of the hypothesis is that it handovers the burden of poor balancing of the work-life as the sole responsibility of employees themselves. The satisfaction hypothesis of work-life balance ignores the influence of societal as well as organisational factors in facilitating an environment for employees in balancing their work with personal life (Carlson, Grzywacz, & Zivnuska, Is work–family balance more than conflict and enrichment?, 2009).

2.1.3 Role conflict hypothesis of work-life balance

Role conflict hypothesis of work-life (family) balance was proposed by Sue Campbell Clark (2000). Clark (2000) defined work-life (family) balance as a state at which an employee experience least level of role conflict among various life domains. However, Clark (2000) narrow down the life as the replication of family and thereby defined work-life balance on the basis of the magnitude of friction between work and family domain.

Critique: - Clark (2000) defined balance as a situation at which the friction between the work and family is at a minimum. Later on, several studies (Brough, Siu, O'Driscoll, & Timmis, 2015; Brougha, et al., 2014; Carlson, Grzywacz, & Zivnuska, Is work–family balance more than conflict and enrichment?, 2009; Poelmans, Odle-Dusseau, & Beham, 2008; Joseph & Sebastian, 2017) invalidated the role (minimum) conflict hypothesis proposed by the Sue Campbell Clark in the year 2000 and found that balance is a concept which is theoretically as well as empirically distinct from level of minimum conflict. Because of the theoretical distinction between the concept of balance and absence of conflict (level of minimum conflict), scales used to measure the level work-life (family) conflict cannot be used to measure the level of work-life (family) balance (Poelmans, Odle-Dusseau, & Beham, 2008). Furthermore, work-life balance is a concept that encompasses the concept of work-family balance (Joseph & Sebastian, 2017). That is, Clark (2000) has narrowly downed the personal life of an employee to the family domain alone. Another prominent argument against conflict hypothesis of work-life balance is that the work-life interaction not only produce conflict between the domains but also produce enrichment/enhancement between the domains and conflict hypothesis of work-life balance pre-dominantly ignores the positive outcome (enrichment/enhancement) of work-life interaction.

2.1.4 Conflict cum enrichment hypothesis of work-life balance

The conflict cum enrichment hypothesis was developed out of the pitfall of the conflict hypothesis of work-life balance that the conflict hypothesis ignores the positive aspect (enrichment/enhancement) of work-life interaction. The proposers of conflict cum enrichment hypothesis of work-life balance argued that work-life interactions can produce conflict as well as enrichment/enhancement simultaneously and therefore, work-life balance is the aggregate effect of work-life conflict and work-life enrichment. The prominent proponents of conflict cum enrichment hypothesis of work-life balance were Morganson, Litano, & O'Neill, 2014; Zhang, et al., 2012; Rantanen, Kinnunen, MaunO, & Tillemann, 2010; Hayman, 2005; Grzywacz & Bass, 2003; Frone, 2003 and Fisher-McAuley, Stanton, Jolton, & Gavin, 2003.

Critique: - Balance is a concept which is theoretically as well as empirically distinct from both conflict and enrichment (Carlson, Grzywacz, & Zivnuska, Is work–family balance more than conflict and enrichment?, 2009; Kalliath & Brough, 2008). Moreover, the measure of balance has the potential to explain the amount of variance beyond either the measure of conflict or the measure of enrichment can explain in various upshot variables such as work satisfaction, family satisfaction, family functioning, organisational commitment, and family functioning (Carlson, Grzywacz, & Zivnuska, Is work–family balance more than conflict and enrichment?, 2009). That is, the concept of balance can not only be distinguished from conflict and enrichment but also can explain additional variance in outcome variables. It validates the claim that work-life balance can't be estimated by either by studying conflict or enrichment. Hence, estimating the level of work-life balance by aggregating the level of work-life conflict and work-life conflict lacks theoretical as well as empirical validity.

2.1.5 Role control hypothesis of work-life balance

Control over life role is the key to work-life balance, higher the control over life roles higher will be the work-life balance and vice versa (Hutcheson, 2012; Fleetwood, 2006). Laissez-fair approach of employee management is the basis of the role control hypothesis, where the employees have the absolute freedom to determine the activities and roles pertaining to them. Therefore, as per the role control hypothesis of work-life balance providing employees with a greater amount of freedom in their roles can enhance the level of work-life balance.

Critique: - According to the theme proposed by the role control hypothesis of work-life balance absolute control over the role should result in the high level of work-life balance. Control over the role and work-life balance doesn't have a proportional relationship in between (Carlson, Grzywacz, & Zivnuska, Is work–family balance more than conflict and enrichment?, 2009). Enhancement of the role control results in the omnipotence of the employee themselves, which ultimately enhance the intra-employee clashes and diminishes the level of work-life balance rather than enhancing the level of work-life balance. Furthermore, the proposers of the role control hypothesis of work-life balance haven't yet validated their conceptual claim empirically that the work-life balance is proportional to role control. Role control is only one of the several elements responsible for work-life balance (Carlson, Grzywacz, & Zivnuska, Is work–family balance more than conflict and enrichment?, 2009; Kalliath & Brough, 2008; Grzywacz & Dawn S.

Carlson, 2007). Hence, defining the work-life balance level as a proportionate consequence of role control is absurd and arbitrary.

2.1.6 Equilibrium demand hypothesis of work-life balance

The prominent proponents of equilibrium demand hypothesis were Kumari & Selvi, 2015; Gananapalli, 2015 and Monica.M, 2015. According to the equilibrium demand hypothesis of work-life balance, work-life balance occurs when the demand arising out of multiple roles across various life domains are similar in nature. That is, equal demand both at the work and at the family is the basis of work-life balance (Kumari & Selvi, 2015). An uneven increase in the demand (increase in the responsibility) either from the work or from the family cause disequilibrium demand and result in a work-life imbalance.

Critique: - Having equal demand across multiple domains can only be considered as a myth and can only be defined conceptually, in practice having parallel demand across multiple domain is an illusion (Schwingshackl, 2014). The individual capability of the employee to adapt in accordance with the environmental situation is the essence of work-life balance (Ingham, 2007). Defining the magnitude of demand from various life domains objectively that can ensure work-life balance is impossible. Work-life balance is possible only through the conscious effort of an individual (Raja & Stein, 2014). Furthermore, domain demand is depended on time and environment. That is, based on the changes in the time and living environment the demand exerted by the life domains varies significantly. The work-life imbalance burst out when the employee is incapable to adapt his behaviours in accordance with the change in the living environment (domain demands) (Kong, 2015). The equilibrium demand hypothesis quashes all the influence of individualistic capabilities and resources in balancing the work-life. Defining work-life balance as a concept of equilibrium demand, the burden of work-life balance is the sole responsibility of the employer and the society as a whole and thereby releasing the employee responsibility in balancing the life in between personal life and professional life.

2.1.7 Time management hypothesis of work-life balance

Time management hypothesis of work-life balance states that work-life balance time management is the key to work-life balance. In order to have work-life balance in life, an employee should apportionment the time between various life domains. The absence of time to carry out the domain role functions results in work-life imbalance through role stress and strain. As per time management hypothesis of work-life balance, employee preserves ample time for each and every life domain enjoy the maximum work-life balance level. The prominent scholars who backs time management hypothesis of work-life balance were Jindal, 2016; Bruton, 2012; Ervin, 2012 and State Services Commission New Zealand, 2005.

Critique: - Apportionment of time across various life domains doesn't ensure a balance between work and personal life (Valcour, 2007). The literature on work-life balance showed that there is no consistency among studies, that explore the relationship between work-life balance and time. Monica.M (2015) found that there is no relationship between time management and work-life balance. Another drawback of the time management hypothesis of work-life balance is that the work-life balance scholars failed to validate the model empirically. However, it is found that there are either negative or zero relationships between hours of work and work-life balance (Valcour, 2007; Clarke, Koach, & Hill, 2004; White, Hill, McGovern, Mills, & Smeaton, 2003; Hill, Hawkins, Ferris, & Weitzman, 2001). That is, the relationship between time management and work-life balance is arbitrary in nature. According to Smith and Gardner (2007), time demand is only one of the several factors that influence the employee level of work-life balance.

2.1.8 Perception hypothesis of work-life balance

Thomas Kalliath and Paula Brough (2008) founded the perception hypothesis of work-life balance. According to the perception based hypothesis of work-life balance, work-life balance is the subjective perception of the employee themselves with regard to the compatibleness of their work and non-work activities in comparison with their perception about the ideal state of work-life balance. Subjective evaluation about the self with regard to the compatibility between the work and non-work activities in view of the ideal is the core theme of the perception based hypothesis of work-life balance. The concept of balance has been distinguished from conflict and enrichment during the very beginning of the 21st century itself. Hill, Hawkins, Ferris, & Weitzman (2001) proposed a model of work-family balance that inculculates the time effect, role demand, and individual perception about the balancing between work and family roles. However, the model put forward by the Hill, Hawkins, Ferris, & Weitzman (2001) narrow downed the personal life to family alone. The prominent scholars who support perception based hypothesis of work-life balance were Hill, Hawkins, Ferris, & Weitzman (2001), Valcour (2007), Kalliath and Brough

(2008), Brougha, et al., (2014), Schwingshackl, 2014), and Brough, Siu, O'Driscoll, & Timmis, (2015).

Critique: **-** Perception hypothesis of work-life balance is based on employee perception about the balance between work life and personal life. The perception hypothesis of work-life balance successfully distinguished the concept of balance from conflict and enrichment (see Brougha, et al., 2014; Schwingshackl, 2014; Carlson, Grzywacz, & Zivnuska, 2009, and Kalliath & Brough, 2008 for more details). The construct of balance has the potential to explain variance beyond the construct of conflict and enrichment can explain in outcome variables such as family satisfaction, job satisfaction, family performance, family functioning, and organisational commitment (Carlson, Grzywacz, & Zivnuska, Is work–family balance more than conflict and enrichment?, 2009). Which means, the construct of balance not only can inculculate the content of conflict and enrichment construct but also can explain additional variance in work, family, and personal life domains.

Furthermore, Joseph and Sebastian (in press) empirically validated that conceptual perception that work-life balance is a concept work-life balance is a concept which is different from work-family balance. That is, narrow downing the concept of work-life balance to work-family balance is conceptually as well as empirically invalid. While considering the scope of work-life balance and work-family balance, Joseph and Sebastian (2017) found that the construct of work-life balance can explain variance beyond the construct of work-family balance can explain in work, family, and personal life domain related variables of an employee.

It has been theoretically as well as empirically validated that work-life balance is a construct which is theoretically as well as empirically distinct from work-life conflict, work-life enrichment, synergy of conflict and enrichment, equilibrium demand across domain, equal involvement, time management and freedom of domain control (Brough, Siu, O'Driscoll, & Timmis, 2015; Brougha, et al., 2014; Schwingshackl, 2014; Carlson, Grzywacz, & Zivnuska, Is work–family balance more than conflict and enrichment?, 2009; Kalliath & Brough, 2008; Poelmans, Odle-Dusseau, & Beham, 2008; Grzywacz & Dawn S. Carlson, 2007; Smith & Gardner, 2007; Valcour, 2007; Clarke, Koach, & Hill, 2004). Work-life balance is the self-assessment of an individual about how successfully 'he' fulfil the varying demand across the domain (Valcour, 2007). That is the Kalliath and Brough (2008) definition of work-life is consistent with that of Valcour (2007) definition of work-life balance satisfaction. And is superior to Valcour (2007) definition of work-life satisfaction as there no scope for victim blaming (Carlson, Grzywacz, & Zivnuska, Is work–family balance more than conflict and enrichment?, 2009). Similarly, the Kalliath and Brough definition of work-life balance is well founded theoretically on the role balance theory of Marks & MacDermid (1996) that role balance is more than just low level of role conflict and will result in the superior functioning both at psychological as well as physical level.

Another superiority of the Kalliath and Brough (2008) definition of work-life balance in comparison with other definitions of work-life balance (e.g., G.Grzywacz & S.Carlson, 2007) is ability to conceptualise and synchronise the subjectivity objectively (self-perception about work to non-work balance) with psycho-social factors without negotiating the dynamism (role silence preferred by the individual) of the concept.

2.2 Work-Life Balance Constructs

Work-life balance constructs are those set of tools and techniques on the basis of which work-life balance is estimated quantitatively. On the basis of the methodology adopted with regard to work-life balance estimation. Work-life balance constructs can be broadly classified into two. Work-Family Based Constructs and Work-Nonwork Based Constructs (can be termed as work-personal life based constructs or even as work-life based constructs). Work-Family Based Constructs are those measures of work-life balance founded on the basis of the narrow frame view of work-life balance (i.e., the methodology of understanding work-life balance through the study of work-family domain interaction alone). Whereas the Work-Nonwork Based Constructs are those measures of work-life balance founded on the basis of the broad frame view of work-life balance (i.e., is the methodology of understanding work-life balance through the study of the interaction between work with all the other non-work related activities that are relevant to an individual). In the realm of work-life balance research, from its early conceptualisation itself, there was a conflict with regard to the conceptual clarity about the work-life balance construct in terms of its scope (i.e., whether there is any theoretical distinction between work-family balance and work-life balance) (Joseph & Sebastian, in press). Therefore, based on each view of work-life balance, distinctive work-life balance estimation approaches have been evolved.

2.2.1 Work-life balance – approaches and measurements

On the basis of the methodology adopted to study and estimate the work-life balance. Work-life balance studies can be classified into two. Narrow Frame View of Work-Life Balance (NFVWLB) and Broad Frame View of Work-Life Balance (BFVWLB). Narrow frame view of work-life balance is the methodology of understanding work-life balance through the study of work-family domain interaction alone. Whereas the broad frame view of work-life balance is the methodology of understanding work-life balance through the study of work-to-non-work (personal life) domain interaction. In the realm of work-life balance research, from its early conceptualisation itself there was a conflict with regard to the conceptual clarity about the work-life balance construct in terms of its scope (i.e., whether there is any theoretical distinction between work-family balance and work-life balance). Therefore, each view (NFVWLB as well as BFVWLB) has its own separate methods for estimating work-life balance based on each of the work-life balance definition.

2.2.2 NFVWLB vs. BFVWLB

The advocates of narrow frame (e.g., Dhanya & Kinslin, 2017; Gehrke & Hassard, 2015; G.Grzywacz & S.Carlson, 2007; Wayne, Grzywacz, Carlson, & Kacmar, 2007; Wayne, Musisca, & Fleeson, 2004; Allen, Herst, Bruck, & Sttton, 2000; Clark, 2000; Frone, Russell, & Cooper, 1992; Barling, 1986; Staines, 1980; Holahan & Gilbert, 1979) argue that is no significant conceptual distinction between work-family-balance construct and work-life balance construct. According to narrow frame advocates, work-life balance means the balance between work and personal life. Where personal life is the replica of family life and therefore work-life balance is the replica of work-family balance and therefore work-family balance construct and work-life balance construct can be considered as identical.

On the other hand, the advocates of broad frame (Smeltzer, et al., 2016; Brough, et al., 2014; Fisher, Bulger, & Smith, 2009; Kalliath & Brough, 2008; Hayman, 2005; Fisher-McAuley, Stanton, Jolton, & Gavin, 2003; Frone, 2003; Cohen, 1997; Kirchmeyer, 1995; Kirchmeyer, Nonwork Participation and Work Attitudes: A Test of Scarcity vs. Expansion Models of Personal Resources, 1992; Kirchmeyer, Perceptions of Nonwork-to-Work Spillover: Challenging the Common View of Conflict-Ridden Domain Relationships, 1992) argue that work-family balance construct and work-life balance cannot be considered identical. Where the personal life indoctrinates domains other than family; such as self, society, friends and other affiliated groups (religion, community, political affiliation etc..,). Therefore, work-family balance can only be a subset of work-life balance and hence there is conceptual independence between these constructs. The following table illustrates the construct wise classification of work-life balance estimation technique.

Table 2.2

Work-Life Balance Measurement Constructs

Construct Dimensions	Work-Family Based Constructs (based on narrow frame view of work-life balance)		Work-Nonwork Based Constructs (based on broad frame view of work-life balance)
Conflict based approach of	Work-family (life) balance is a situation at which when there is a low level of work-	Core theme	Low level of work to non-work (personal life) conflict (work-personal life as well

work-life balance	family conflict (work-family as well as family-work)		as personal life-work) is considered as the state of work-life balance
	White, Hill, McGovern, Mills, & Smeaton (2003); Major, Klein, & Ehrhart (2002); Clerk (2000); Saltzstein, Ting, & Saltzstein (2001); Allen, Herst, Bruck, & Sttton (2000); Deckman (1996); Staines & O'Connor (1980) Carlson, Kacmar, & Williams (2000) scale of work-family conflict; Netemeyer et al., (1996) scale of work-family conflict; Stephens & Sommer (1996) scale of work-family conflict; Frone, Russell & Cooper (1992) scale of work-family conflict; Kopelman, Greenhaus, & Connolly (1983) scale of work-family conflict	*Proposer(s)*	Department of Labour New Zealand (2006); Tausig & Fenwick (2001); Hobson, Delunas, & Kesic (2001); Rice, Frone, & McFarlin (1992)
		Most widely used measures	Tausig & Fenwick (2001) scale of work-life balance; Rice, Frone, & McFarlin (1992) scale of work-nonwork conflict;
	21st century researches (eg., G.Grzywacz & S.Carlson, 2007; Carlson, Grzywacz, & Zivnuska 2009) theoretically as well as empirically validated that work-family conflict is a construct distinct from work-	*Critique*	Researchers have arrived at the conscience that work-life conflict is a construct distinct from work-life balance (Kossek & Lee, 2017; Dulk, Groeneveld, Ollier-Malaterre, &

		Core theme		Proposer(s)		Most widely used measures		Critique

Enrichment based approach of work-life balance	family balance. That is it is not possible to estimate the work-family balance level through measuring work-family conflict. High level of work-family enrichment (work-family as well as family-work) is considered as the state of work-family (life) balance	*Core theme*	Valcour, 2013). Therefore, estimating the work-life balance based on the work-life conflict level is invalid and should be avoided. High level of work-personal life enrichment (work-personal life as well as personal life-work) is considered as the state of work-life balance
	Kacmar, Crawford, Carlson, Ferguson, & Whitten (2014); Carlson, Kacmar, Wayne, & Grzywacz (2006); Greenhaus and Powell (2006); Rothbrad (2000); Branett & Hyde, (2001) Kacmar, Crawford, Carlson, Ferguson, & Whitten (2014) scale of work-family enrichment; Carlson, Kacmar, Wayne, & Grzywacz (2006) scale of work-family enrichment; Hanson et al., (2006) scale of work to family positive spillover; Wayne et al., (2004) scale of work-family facilitation	*Proposer(s)*	Ruderman, Ohlott, Panzer, & King (2002)
		Most widely used measures	Ruderman, Ohlott, Panzer, & King (2002) personal to professional life enhancement scale; Tiedje et al., (1990) role enhancemnt scale
	Work-family enrichment is a	*Critique*	Work-life enrichment

		Core theme	
	construct which is theoretically (G.Grzywacz & S.Carlson, 2007) as well as empirically (Carlson, Grzywacz, & Zivnuska, Is work–family balance more than conflict and enrichment?, 2009) distinct from work-life balance. Hence, estimating work-family balance based on work-family enrichment will only be a handicapped approach.		(enhancement/facilit ation/spillover) is only a factor that can be a facilitator (depending upon the environmental situation) of work-life balance (Nabong & Trønnes, 2016). Therefore, it is invalid to ascertain work-life balance based on the level of work-life enrichment.
Approach of synergy	Low level of work-family conflict (work-family as well as family-work) together with a high level of work-family enrichment (work-family as well as family-work) is regarded as work-family (life) balance	Core theme	Low level of work-personal life conflict (work-personal life as well as personal life-work) together with a high level of work-personal life enrichment (work-personal life as well as personal life-work) is regarded as work-life balance Hayman (2005); Fisher-McAuley, Stanton, Jolton, & Gavin (2003); Fisher (2000); Grzywacz & Marks (2000)
	Aryee, Srinivas, & Hwee (2005); Hammer, Cullen, B, Sinclair, & Shafiro (2005); Grzywacz (2000)	Proposer(s)	
	Aryee, Srinivas, & Hwee (2005) scale of work-family balance; Hammer, Cullen, B, Sinclair, & Shafiro	Most widely used measures	Hyman (2005) scale of work-personal life balance; Fisher (2000) scale of work-life balance;

	(2005) scale of work-family spillover; Grzywacz (2000) work-family spillover scale;		Grzywacz & Marks (2000) scale of work-life spillover
	Several studies (G.Grzywacz & S.Carlson, 2007; Carlson, Grzywacz, & Zivnuska, Is work–family balance more than conflict and enrichment?, 2009) has proved that work-family enrichment and work-family conflict were distinct from work-family balance. That is, it is not possible through estimate work-family balance through aggregating the total effect of work-family enrichment and work-family conflict.	*Critique*	Several studies (Brough, Siu, O'Driscoll, & Timmis, 2015; Kalliath & Brough, 2008; Hill, Hawkins, Ferris, & Weitzman, 2001) have validated (both theoretically as well empirically) that effect of domain spillover (aggregating conflict and enrichment) can't predict the level of work-life balance. Therefore, the estimation of work-life balance through aggregating the work-personal life conflict and enrichment is void.
Satisfaction based approach of work-life balance	Work-family (life) balance is the achievement of satisfying experience across work and family domain.	*Core theme*	Work-life balance is the achievement of satisfying experience across all life domain.
	Valcour (2007)	*Proposer(s)*	Kirchmeyer (2000); Kofodimos (1993) Shanafelt, et al. (2012) satisfaction with work-life balance scale.
	Valcour (2007) scale of work-family balance.	*Most widely used measures*	

Domain (role) balance based approach of work-life balance	Satisfaction across work-family domain is a construct which is distinct from work-family balance (G.Grzywacz & S.Carlson, 2007). The concept of satisfaction across the domain (work-family) is vague and practically elusive (Carlson, Grzywacz, & Zivnuska, 2009). Therefore, it is void to interpret work-family domain satisfaction as work-family balance.	*Critique*	Brough, et al. (2014) argued that satisfaction based measure of work life balance are dependent in nature. Lack of predictive power diminishes the utility of the construct as the work-life balance estimation has got only very limited applications. That is satisfaction based work-life balance estimation has got sever drawbacks.
	Work-family (life) balance is the accomplishment of role related expectations across work and family domain.	*Core theme*	Work-life balance is the perception about balance across various life domain in such a way that promote growth together with role silence.
	Carlson, Grzywacz, & Zivnuska (2009); G.Grzywacz & S.Carlson (2007); Milkie & Peltola (1999)	*Proposer(s)*	Brough et al., (2014); Kalliath and Brough (2008); Hill, Hawkins, Ferris, & Weitzman (2001); Hill, Miller, Weiner, & Colihan (1998)
	Carlson, Grzywacz, & Zivnuska (2009) scale of work-family balance; Marks & MacDermid (1996) sale of role balance.	*Most widely used measures*	Brough et al., (2014) scale of work-life balance; Hill, Hawkins, Ferris, & Weitzman (2001) scale of work-life balance

	Critique	
The construct emphasised the relational aspect work-family domain and exclude the psychological aspect (Casper, Vaziri, Wayne, DeHauw, & Greenhaus, 2017; Brough, et al., 2014). Domain balance theme of the work-life balance construct make it more elusive as it is influenced by multiplicity of factors and similarly the exclusion of psychological element makes the construct objective towards expectations of an individual rather than current appraisal of the existing situation.		The construct provides the subjective evaluation of the current state of balance across various life domains (not limited to work and family). Another advantage of this construct is that it gives due consideration for both psychological as well as social factors.

As illustrated in table 2.1 the domain balance approach under work-nonwork based construct is the best available approach towards the measurement of work-life balance. The most commonly used (theoretically validated) work-life balance measurement scale under this approach was Brough et al., (2014) scale of work-life balance and Hill, Hawkins, Ferris, & Weitzman (2001) scale of work-life balance. In comparison with Hill, Hawkins, Ferris, & Weitzman (2001) scale of work-life balance, Brough et al., (2014) scale of work-life balance has the following advantages.

1. Brough et al., (2014) scale have been developed on the basis of rigorous cross-sectional and longitudinal validation with a fairly large sample size of 6983 from Australia, New Zealand, China, and Taiwan. Whereas the work-life balance scale of Hill, Hawkins, Ferris, & Weitzman (2001) has not been evaluated longitudinally.

2. Brough et al., (2014) scale have been found valid in terms of its convergent and divergent validity. Where in the case of Hill, Hawkins, Ferris, & Weitzman (2001) scale of work-life balance no such information is available.

3. Brough et al., (2014) scale of work-life balance is well founded on the Kalliath and Brough (2008) theoretical definition of work-life balance. Whereas Hill, Hawkins, Ferris, & Weitzman (2001) failed to define the theoretical framework (definition) on the basis of which the construct has been developed.

Therefore, it is very clear that Brough et al (2014) scale of work-life balance has a superiority over Hill, Hawkins, Ferris, & Weitzman (2001) scale of work-life balance in terms of its underlying theoretical framework and validity. And because of this comparative advantage of Brough et al., (2014) scale of work-life balance over Hill, Hawkins, Ferris, & Weitzman (2001) scale of work-life balance, Brough et al., (2014) scale has been used in this study in order to measure the work-life balance level of the respondents.

References

Ajay KR, S., & Amanjot, S. (2012). Work Life Balance and Subjective Well Being: A Comparative Study in Public and Private Institutes in Higher Education.

Allen, T. D., Herst, D. E., Bruck, C. S., & Sttton, M. (2000). Consequences Associated With Work-to-Family Conflict:A Review and Agenda for Future Research. *Journal of Occupational Health Psychology, 5*(2), 278-308. doi:10.1037//1076-8998.5.2.278

Aryee, S., Srinivas, E. S., & Hwee, H. (2005). Rhythms of Life: Antecedents and Outcomes of Work-Family Balance in Employed Parents. *Journal of Applied Psychology, 90*(1), 132-138.

Barling, J. (1986). Interrole conflict and marital functioning amongst employed fathers. *Journal of Organizational Behavior*, 61-66. doi:10.1002/job.4030070108

Branett, R. C., & Hyde, J. S. (2001). Women, Men, Work and Family: An Expansionist Theory. *American Psychologist*, 781-796.

Brough, P., Siu, O. L., O'Driscoll, M., & Timmis, C. (2015). Work–family enrichment and satisfaction: The mediating role of self-efficacy and work–life balance . *The International Journal of Human Resource Management*. doi:10.1080/09585192.2015.1075574

Brough, P., Timmsb, C., O'Driscollc, M. P., Kalliathd, T., Siue, O.-L., Sitf, C., & Log, D. (2014, March). Work–life balance: a longitudinal evaluation of a new measure across Australia and New Zealand workers. *The International Journal of Human Resource Management, 25*(19), 2724-2744. doi:10.1080/09585192.2014.899262

Brougha, P., Timmsb, C., O'Driscollc, M. P., Kalliathd, T., Siue, O.-L., Sitf, C., & Log, D. (2014, March). Work–life balance: a longitudinal evaluation of a new measure across Australia and New Zealand workers. *The International Journal of Human Resource Management, 25*(19), 2724-2744. doi:10.1080/09585192.2014.899262

Bruton, A. (2012). *Work Life Balance and the Workforce Reforms.* PhD Thesis, University of Birmingham, School of Education, Birmingham.

Carlson, D. S., Grzywacz, J. G., & Zivnuska, S. (2009, October). Is work–family balance more than conflict and enrichment? *National Institute of Health, 62*(10), 1-20. doi:10.1177/0018726709336500

Carlson, D. S., Kacmar, K. M., & Williams, L. J. (2000). Construction and Initial Validation of a Multidimensional Measure of Work–Family Conflict. *Journal of Vocational Behavior, 56*, 249-276. doi:10.1006/jvbe.1999.1713

Casper, W. J., Vaziri, H., Wayne, J. H., DeHauw, S., & Greenhaus, J. (2017). The Jingle-Jangle of Work–Nonwork Balance: A Comprehensive and Meta-Analytic Review of Its Meaning and Measurement. *Journal of Applied Psychology*. doi:10.1037/apl0000259

Chandarasekar, K. S., S, S., Nair, R. S., & S.R, A. (2013). Study on Work-Life Balance among the executives in IT Industry with special reference to Technopark, Trivandrum, Kerala. *Asian Journal of Multidimensional Research, 2*(3).

Clark, S. C. (2000). Work/Family Border Theory: A New Theory of Work/Family Balance. *Human Relations*, 747-770. doi:10.1177/0018726700536001

Clarke, M. C., Koach, L. C., & Hill, E. J. (2004). The Work-Family Interface: Differentiating Balance and Fit. *Family and Consumer Sciences Research Journal, 23*(2), 121-140. doi:10.1177/1077727X04269610

Deckman, M. E. (1996). Balancing Work and Family Responsibilities: Flextime and Child Care in the Federal Government. *Public Administration Review, 56*(2), 174-179. doi:10.2307/977205

Dhanya.J.S, & Kinslin, D. (2017, January 30). *A study on work life balance of women employees at ULCCS Ltd, Kozhkode*. Retrieved from Resrarchgate.net: https://www.researchgate.net/publication

Dulk, L. d., Groeneveld, S., Ollier-Malaterre, A., & Valcour, M. (2013). National context in work-life research: A multi-level cross-national analysis of the adoption of workplace work-life arrangements in Europe. *uropean Management Journal*, 478-496.

Edwards, J. R., & Rothbard, N. P. (2000). Mechanisms linking Work and Family: Clarifying the relationhip between Work and Family Constructs. *Academy of Management Review, 25*(1), 178-199.

Ervin, S. M. (2012). *A Comparative Analysis of Work-Life Balance in Intercollegiate Athletic Graduate Assistants and Supervisors.* Georgia State University, Department of Kinesiology and Health. Georgia: Georgia State University. Retrieved from http://scholarworks.gsu.edu

Fisher-McAuley, G., Stanton, J. M., Jolton, J. A., & Gavin, J. (2003). Modeling the Relationship between Work/Life Balance and Organizational Outcomes. 1-30. Retrieved August 8, 2016, from https://www.researchgate.net/publication/260516221

Fleetwood, S. (2006). *Why work-life balance now?* Lancaster: Lancaster University Management School.

Frone, M. R. (2003). Work-family balance. In *Handbook of occupational health psychology* (pp. 143-162). Washington: American Psychological Association.

Frone, M. R., Russell, M., & Cooper, M. L. (1992). Antecedents and Outcomes of Work-Family Conflict: Testing a Model of the Work-Family Interface. *Journal of Applied Psychology, 77*(1), 65-78. doi:10.1037//0021-9010.77.1.65

G.Grzywacz, J., & S.Carlson, D. (2007, November). Conceptualizing Work–Family Balance: Implications for Practice and Research. *Advances in Developing Human Resources, 9*(4), 455-471. doi:10.1177/1523422307305487

G.Shiva. (2013). A Study on Work Family Balance and Challenges Faced By Working Women. *IOSR Journal of Business and Management, 14*(5), 1-4. Retrieved from www.iosrjournals.org

Gananapalli, S. (2015). *Work Life Balance of Women Employees in State Bank of India.* PhD Thesis, Sri Krishnadevaraya Institute of Management, Anantapur.

Gehrke, A., & Hassard, J. (2015, January 26). *Work-life balance – Managing the interface between family and working life.* Retrieved from OSH WIKI: https://oshwiki.eu/wiki/Work-life_balance_Managing_the_interface_between_family_and_working_lif e

Greenhaus, J. H., & Powell, G. N. (2006). When the Work and Family are Allies: A Theory of Work-Family Enrichment. *Academy of Management Review, 31*(1), 72-92.

Greenhaus, J. H., & Singh, R. (2004). Work and Family, Relationship between. In C. Spielberger, *Encyclopedia of Applied Psychology* (pp. 687-697). New York: Academic Press.

Greenhaus, J. H., Collins, K. M., & Shaw, J. D. (2003). The relation between work-life balance and quality of life. *Journal of Vocational Behavior*, 510-531. doi:10.1016/S0001-8791(02)00042-8

Grzywacz, J. G. (2000). Work-Family Spillover and Health During Midlife: Is Managing Conflict Everything? *The Science of Health Promotion*, 236-243.

Grzywacz, J. G., & Bass, B. L. (2003). Work, family, and mental health: Testing different models of work-family fit. *Journal of Marriage and Family*, 248-261.

Grzywacz, J. G., & Marks, N. F. (2000). Family, Work, Work-Family Spillover, and Problem Drinking During Midlife. *Journal of Occupational Health Psychology*, 111-126.

Grzywacz, J., & Dawn S. Carlson. (2007, November). Conceptualizing Work–Family Balance: Implications for Practice and Research. *Advances in Developing Human Resources, 9*(4), 455-471. doi:10.1177/1523422307305487

Hammer, L. B., Cullen, J. C., B, N. M., Sinclair, R. R., & Shafiro, M. V. (2005). The longitudinal effects of work-family conflict and positive spillover on depressive symptoms among dual-earner couples. *Journal of Occupational Health Psychology, 10*(2), 138-154.

Hayman, J. (2005). Psychometric Assessment of an Instrument Designed to Measure Work Life Balance. *Research and Practice in Human Resource Management*, 85-91.

Hill, E. J., Hawkins, A. J., Ferris, M., & Weitzman, M. (2001). Finding an Extra Day a Week: The Positive Influence of Perceived Job Flexibility on Work and Family Life Balance. *Family Relations*, 49-58.

Hill, E. J., Miller, B. C., Weiner, S. P., & Colihan, J. (1998). Influences of the virtual office on aspects of work and work/life balance. *Personnel Psychology, 51*(3), 667-683.

Hobson, C. J., Delunas, L., & Kesic, D. (2001). Compelling evidence of the need for corporate work/life balance initiatives: results from a national survey of stressful life-events. *Journal of Employment Counseling*, 8-44.

Holahan, C. K., & Gilbert, L. A. (1979). Interrole conflict for working women: Careers versus jobs. *ournal of Applied Psychology*, 86-90. doi:10.1037/0021-9010.64.1.86

Hutcheson, P. G. (2012). *Work-Life Balance.* Georgia: IEEE-USA.

Ingham, G. (2007). *Motivate People Getting the Best from Yourself and Others.* London: Dorling Kindersley Limited .

Jindal, M. (2016). A Study on Work-life Balance of Working Women in Service Sector. *International Journal of Research in Finance and Marketing*, 14-21.

Joseph, J., & Sebastian, D. J. (2017). Work-life balance vs Work-Family Balance - An Evaluation of Scope. *Amity Global HRM Review*, 54-65.

Jyothi, V. S. (2011). *Work-Life Balance among Women employees in Organizations: A Study in Andhra Pradesh.* PhD Thesis, University of Hyderabad, Department of Management, Hyderabad.

Kacmar, K. M., Crawford, W. S., Carlson, D. S., Ferguson, M., & Whitten, D. (2014). A Short and Valid Measure of Work-Family Enrichment. *Journal of Occupational Health Psychology, 19*(1), 32-45. doi:10.1037/a0035123

Kalliath, T., & Brough, P. (2008). Work–life balance: A review of the meaning of the balance construct. *Journal of Management & Organization , 14*(3), 323-327.

Kirchmeyer, C. (1992). Perceptions of Nonwork-to-Work Spillover: Challenging the Common View of Conflict-Ridden Domain Relationships. *Basic and Applied Social Psychology*, 231-249. doi:10.1207/s15324834basp1302_7

Kirchmeyer, C. (1992). Nonwork Participation and Work Attitudes: A Test of Scarcity vs. Expansion Models of Personal Resources. *Human Relations*, 775-795. doi:10.1177/001872679204500802

Kirchmeyer, C. (1995). Managing the Work-Nonwork Boundary: An Assessment of Organizational Responses. *Human Relations*, 515-536. doi:10.1177/001872679504800504

Kirchmeyer, C. (2000). Work-life initiatives: Greed or benevolence regarding workers' time? In *Trends in organizational behavior* (pp. 79-93). New York: John Wiley & Sons Ltd.

Kodz, J., Harper, H., & Dench, S. (2002). *Work-Life Balance: Beyond the Rhetoric.* Brighton: The Institute for Employment Studies. Retrieved from http://www.employment-studies.co.uk

Kofodimos, J. R. (1993). Balancing act: How managers can integrate successful careers and fulfilling personal lives. *The Jossey-Bass management series.*

Kong, M. Y. (2015). Balance is in the Moment. *Frontiers in Pediatrics*, 1-3. doi:10.3389/fped.2015.00087

Kopelman, R. E., Greenhaus, J., & Connolly, T. F. (1983). A model of work, family, and interrole conflict: A construct validation study. *Organizational Behavior & Human Performance*, 198-215.

Kossek, E. E., & Lee, K.-H. (2017). Work-Family Conflict and Work-Life Conflict . *Oxford Research Encyclopedia of Business and Management*, 23-33.

Kumari, S., & Selvi, A. (2015). An Exploratory Study Of Work Life Balance Emanates And Work Satisfaction In Ericsson Company-Chennai City. *International Journal of scientific research and management*, 3565-3570.

Littig, B. (2008). Work Life Balance – catchword or catalyst for sustainable work? *Reihe Soziologie / Sociological Series 85* , 1-14. Retrieved from http://www.ihs.ac.at

Major, V. S., Klein, K. J., & Ehrhart, M. G. (2002). Work Time, Work Interference With Family, and Psychological Distress. *Journal of Applied Psychology, 87*(3), 427-436. doi:10.1037//0021-9010.87.3.427

Malaviya, V. (2012). *Determinants of Work Life Imbalance among Faculty Members of Higher Educational Institutes in Delhi.* Bhagwant University Ajmer, Department of Management, Ajmer.

Marks, S., & MacDermid, S. M. (1996). Multiple Roles and the Self: A Theory of Role Balance. *Journal of Marriage and the Family, 58*(2), 417-432.

Milkie, M. A., & Peltola, P. (1999). Playing All the Roles: Gender and the Work-Family Balancing Act. *Journal of Marriage and the Family, 61*(2), 476-490. Retrieved from http://www.jstor.org/stable/353763

Monica.M. (2015, June). A study on work life balance at State Bank of Mysore. *International Journal of in Multidisciplinary and Academic Research (SSIJMAR), 4*(3), 1-15. Retrieved from www.ssijmar.in

Morganson, V. J., Litano, M. L., & O'Neill, S. K. (2014). Promoting Work–Family Balance Through Positive Psychology: A Practical Review of the Literature. *The Psychologist-Manager Journal, 17*(4), 221-244. doi:10.1037/mgr0000023

Nabong, T., & Trønnes, H. (2016). *A Delicate Balance? A study of work-life conflicts, work-life enrichment, and worklife balance among management consultants in Norway.* Bergen: Norwegian School of Economics Bergen.

Netemeyer, R. G., Boles, J. S., & McMurrian, R. (1996). Development and Validation of Work-Family Conflict and Family-Work Conflict Scales. *Journal of Applied Psychology, 81*(4), 400-410.

Parida, S. K. (2012, June). Measuring the Work Life Balance: An Inter-Personal study of the employees in IT and ITes Scctor. *An International Business Research Journal, 1*(1), 79-90. Retrieved from www.jbmcr.org

Poelmans, S., Odle-Dusseau, H. N., & Beham, B. (2008). Work-life balance: Individual and organizational strategies and practices. In *The Oxford Handbook of Organizational Well Being* (pp. 180-213). Oxford University Press.

Raja, S., & Stein, S. L. (2014). Work–Life Balance: History, Costs, and Budgeting for Balance. *Clinics in Colon and Rectal Surgery, 27*(2), 71-74.

Rajkumar, R. (2014). *Work Life Balance of IT Professionals in Relation to their Self Consept, Hardiness, and Emotional Maturity. .* PhD Thesis, Annamalai University, Department of Business Administration, Annamalai Nagar.

Rantanen, J., Kinnunen, U., MaunO, S., & Tillemann, K. (2010). Introducing Theoretical Approaches to Work-Life Balance and Testing a New Typology Among Professionals. In S. Kaiser, M. J. Ringlstetter, D. R. Eikhof, & M. P. Cunha (Eds.), *Creating Balance?* (pp. 27-46). Springer Berlin Heidelberg. doi:10.1007/978-3-642-16199-5

Redmond, J., Valiulis, M., & Drew, E. (2006). *Literature review of issues related to work-life balance, workplace culture and maternity/childcare issues.* Dublin: Crisis Pregnancy Agency.

Rice, R. W., Frone, M. R., & McFarlin, D. B. (1992). Work-nonwork conflict and the perceived quality of life. *Journal of Organizational Behavior*, 155-168.

Ruderman, M., Ohlott, P., Panzer, K., & King, S. N. (2002). Benefits of Multiple Roles for Managerial Women. *The Academy of Management Journal*, 369-386.

Saltzstein, A. L., Ting, Y., & Saltzstein, G. H. (2001). Work-Family Balance and Job Satisfaction: The Impact of Family-Friendly Policies on Attitudes of Federal Government Employees. *Public Administration Review*, 452-467. doi:10.1111/0033-3352.00049

Schwingshackl, A. (2014). The Fallacy of Chasing after Work-Life Balance. In J. H. Lee, *Frontiers in Pediatrics* (pp. 1-3). Frontiers.

Shanafelt, T. D., Boone, S., Tan, L., Dyrbye, L. N., Sotile, W., Satele, D., . . . Oreskovich, M. R. (2012). Burnout and Satisfaction With Work-Life Balance Among US Physicians Relative to the General US Population. *Arch Intern Med*, 1377-1385. doi:10.1001/archinternmed.2012.3199

Sheokand, K. S., & Priyanka. (2013). Work Life Balance: An Overview of Indian Companies. *International Journal of Research in Commerce and Management*, 138-143.

Smith, J., & Gardner, D. (2007). Factors Affecting Employee Use of Work-Life Balance Initiatives. *New Zealand Journal of Psychology, 32*(1), 3-12.

Sree, G. K. (2013). *Work Life Balance of Employees.* Andhra University, Department of Commerce and Management Studies, Visakhapatnam.

Staines, G. L., & O'Connor, P. (1980). Conflicts among Work, Leisure, and Family Roles. *Monthly Labor Review, 103*(8), 35-39. Retrieved from http://www.jstor.org/stable/41841305

State Services Commission. (2005). *Work-Life Balance: a resource for the State Services.* Wellington, New Zealand: State Services Commission.

Stepanova, O. (2012). *Work-Life Balance in Organizational Subcultures The Case of Mutua.* PhD Thesis, University of Barcelona, Barcelona.

Stephens, G. K., & Sommer, S. M. (1996). The Measurement of Work to Family Conflict. *Educational and Psychological Measurement*, 475-486. doi:10.1177/0013164496056003009

Sunderaraj, R. (2012). *Psychometric Study on Locus of Control and its Magnitude of Influence on Stress and Work Life Balance - With reference to Non*

Gazetted Officers of Coimbatore City Police. Bharathiar University, Commerce.

Swarnalatha, T. (2013). *An Empirical Analysis of work-life balance on Woman Employees: A Study with Reference to Banking Sector at Chennai.* PhD Thesis, Manonmaniam Sundaranar University, Tirunelveli.

Tamsett, J. (2015). The Ultimate Guide to Work/Life Balance. *Optimum Health Magazine* . Analee Matthews.

Tausig, M., & Fenwick, R. (2001). Unbinding Time: Alternate Work Schedules and Work-Life Balance. *Journal of Family and Economic Issues, 22*(2), 101-119.

Tiedje, L. B., Downey, g., & Wortman, C. (1990). Women with Multiple Roles: Role-Compatibility Perceptions, Satisfaction, and Mental Health. *Journal of Marriage and the Family*, 63-72.

Valcour, M. (2007). Work-Based Resources as Moderators of the Relationship Between Work Hours and Satisfaction With Work-Family Balance. *Journal of Applied Psychology, 92*(6), 1512-1523. doi:10.1037/0021-9010.92.6.1512

Viswanathan, K., & Jeyakumaran. (2013, Auguest). Instrument Development for Studying Work Life Balance Programs in Information Technology Firms. *Journal of Business and Management, 11*(4), 47-53. Retrieved from www.iosrjournals.org

Wayne, J. H., Grzywacz, J. G., Carlson, D., & Kacmar, M. (2007). Work-family facilitation: A theoretical explanation and model of primary antecedents and consequences. *Human Resource Management Review*, 63-76. doi:10.1016/j.hrmr.2007.01.002

Wayne, J. H., Musisca, N., & Fleeson, W. (2004). Considering the role of personality in the work-family experience: Relationships of the Big Five to work-family conflict and facilitation. *Journal of Vocational Behavior*, 108-130. doi:10.1016/S0001-8791(03)00035-6

White, M., Hill, S., McGovern, P., Mills, C., & Smeaton, D. (2003). 'High-performance' Management Practices, Working Hours and Work–Life Balance. *British Journal of Industrial Relations*, 175-195.

Yadav, T., & Rani, S. (2015). Work life balance: challenges and opportunities. *International Journal of Applied Research*, 680-684.

Zhang, H., Yip, P. S., Chi, P., Chan, K., Cheung, Y. T., & Zhang, X. (2012). Factor Structure and Psychometric Properties of the Work-Family Balance Scale in an Urban Chinese Sample. *Soc Indic Res*, 409-418. doi:10.1007/s11205-010-9776-3

CHAPTER - 3

REVIEW - DISSERTATIONS

"Ambiguity is very interesting in writing; it's not very interesting in science"

- Junna Levin (Cosmologist)

Theses and dissertations were the best choices for the literature review (Alkhatib, 2013; see also Bruckner, 2013; Whitehead, 2013). Though reviewing these sources requires much time and effort, it can supply information which is more reliable as well as credible as compared to other sources of information (Ramachandran, 2013). The doctoral degree is the most valuable asset that an academician can have (Kharkongor, 2016). Reviewing of doctoral thesis equip one to have a grass root level understanding about the topic under discussion. Academic research lay down the cornerstone for further investigation. Doctoral thesis was embedded with quality based data and is a very prominent source of information as well as intellectual component (Vijayakumar & Vijayakumar, 2007). Table 3.1, illustrates various dissertations that had alley with the concept of work-life balance were presented chronologically in the order of descending.

Table 3.1			
Table Showing the Summary of Dissertations Reviewed			
No.	Study & Type	Sample	Major findings
1	(Cioffi, 2018) Qualitative (QL)	10 private college presidents and an executive coach from New England.	Work-life balance is a matter of concern for private college presidents and the support from the significant others, colleagues and family is very essential for the wellbeing.
2	(Jones, 2018) QL	15 women real estate brokers from California, U.S.A.	Work-life balance coping strategies were proactiveness, commitment, social skills, resilient, participative attitude, and competition.
3	(Bauer, 2017) QT	119 respondents from Amazon Mechanical Turk, U.S.	Work-life balance culture doesn't have any significant influence either on organizational attractiveness or on job pursuit intention. Whereas, work schedule flexibility and employee inducements fount to have an influence on organisational attractiveness and job pursuit intention.
4	(Isdell, 2016) QL	15 mid-career, female, student affairs administrators, U.S.	Work blurring into family and family blurring into work is very common among the respondents and helps to maintain the balance between work and non-work activities. Time management, sharing, and management of family schedule, the delegation of work and socialising were the commonly adopted strategies by the respondents to achieve work-life balance.

5	(Mahajan, 2016) Quantitative (QT)	347 Duel Carrier couples in Pune City, India.	Majority of the respondents (51%) were able to balance their life between work and family domain. Job satisfaction (JS), hours of work and career development have a relationship with WLB. Socialisation helps in developing a good relationship among employees and facilitate the exchange of information between the employees themselves.
6	(Martin, 2016) QT	22 Norwegian women from Norway.	The study found that a supportive relationship and autonomy as the major contributor towards gender equality and work-life balance. The researcher further identifies the employee intelligence as the core factor that influences the magnitude of a supportive relationship, autonomy and gender equality.
7	(Olund, 2016) Qualitative (QL)	14 full-time employees from a U.S. based organisation	Increased workload (workplace email) results in decreased job performance and productivity. Similarly, increased workload results in decreased work-life balance and increased stress. Virtual working helps to impart flexibility and thereby enhance productivity and job performance.
8	(Triplett, 2016) QL	20 Female Adjunct Faculty from community colleges at	Self-motivation and relationship intimacy plays an important role in achieving work-life balance. Because of the nature of their job, adjunct

		Southern California, U.S.	faculty exhibits a higher level of adaptability and it helps them to attain work-life balance.
9	(Ufoegbune, 2016) QL	20 Nigerian woman leaders identified through snowball sampling.	Support and influence from the family was the major source of support in balancing work with personal life.
10	(Farkiya, 2015) QT	200 allopathic doctors from Indore, India.	The major cause of imbalance was physical and mental stress, personal needs and time management, workload and family support and the work Itself. The work-life imbalance has an inverse relationship with performance, morale, and satisfaction. Physical and mental stress can predict work-life imbalance and organisational wellness significantly.
11	(Gananapalli, 2015) QT	523 SBI employees, Rayalaseema, India.	Majority of the respondents (82%) were satisfied with the current WLB policies. WLB has no relationship with age, designation, and location. Employee performance fount to have a relationship with WLB.
12	(Gowgisk, 2015) QT	200 employees, IT and manufacturing, Bengaluru, India.	Sector of employment (manufacturing and IT) and WLB are independent of each other. WLB has a positive correlation with age and experience. Whereas WLB has a negative correlation with

			occupational stress and personal life stress.
13	(Jhamat, 2015) QT	1500-woman professionals from northern India.	72.17 percent of the respondents (doctor-have the highest level of WLB, engineer, lawyer, and teacher) reported having a good WLB level. Personal values and WLB were related. There was no relationship between the profession and social values, religious values, democratic values, aesthetic values, knowledge values, and power values.
14	(Lakshmi K. , 2015) QT	606 nursing staff Chennai, India.	Found that policies such as flexible time arrangements, socialisation, women supportive measures, perks, insurance, and pension can promote WLB.
15	(Sengupta, 2015) QT	200 employees from service sector, Pune, India.	Age, gender, and marital status have a relationship with WLB. Furthermore, the relationship between WLB and career successfulness has a relationship with employee demographics.
16	(Shahisaman, 2015) QL	20 Women working in the field of finance, India.	Classified work-life balance strategies of Indian women into nine classes viz., family perception, independence, education, women empowerment, work strategies, religion, mentor, meaningful work, and self-care.

17	(Varghese, 2015) QT	584 bank employees, Mumbai, India.	Factors such as compensation, social needs, time management, and teamwork have a relationship with employee WLB. Furthermore, the study found that the WLB has a relationship with role satisfaction and health.
18	(Jena, 2014) QT	337 nursing staff, Orissa.	Found that nursing staff has poor WLB level. The level of work as well as the level of personal satisfaction were also low for nursing staff. The WLB level doesn't exhibit any relationship with socio-demographic variables such as income, family type, and social status.
19	(Kaur R. , 2014) QT	432 employees Rail Coach factory, Kapurthala. Punjab, India.	Respondents were dissatisfied with the current WLB policies in operation. The researcher founds that the counselling helps not only to reduce the stress but also helps to develop a positive work attitude among the employees.
20	(Mirji, 2014) QT	350 bank employees in Pune, India.	Only minority (21.47%) of the respondents face the problem of work-life imbalance. Compared to clerk's and bank officers are unable to have work-life balance. Demographic variables such as gender and marital status have relationship with WLB.
21	(Prassadh, 2014) QT	598 employees from BPO,	Factors affecting WLB were organisational commitment, job satisfaction, job stress,

		Tamil Nadu (TN), India	absenteeism, job performance, and Job embeddedness.
22	(Rajkumar, 2014) QT	623 IT professionals from Chennai, India.	WLB has a positive relationship with organisational support. Variables such as age, educational qualification, number of dependents, gender, marital status, and family status have a relationship with WLB. There's a difference in employee opinion before and after training with regard to WLB, organisational support, emotional maturity, and hardness level. Compared to the pre-training opinion, the post-training opinion on WLB level was high.
23	(Rothberg, 2014) QL	20 Women cancer survivors identified from the Digital Women's Project.	Cancer results changes in the outlook and mind-set of the patients. They will become more proactive or reactive the circumstances. The enhanced motivation, ability to take challenges and being focused on nurturing important relationships help them to achieve work-life balance.
24	(Shah, 2014) Mixed	130 and 84 managerial staff from Germany and India respectively.	There is no discrepancy among German and Indian managers with regard to work-life balance strategy, despite the fact that the Indian managers take up every job/role that is offered. Respondents are of opinion that work-life balance is very essential for career advancement. Barriers against

			work-life balance can be clustered into five viz., personal, work-related, social, technological and infrastructural.
25	(Susi.S, 2014) QT	494 IT professionals from Bangalore city, India.	Respondents reported having good WLB level based on the mean score obtained on WLB scale (Fisher, 2001 scale of WLB). Age and gender have a relationship with WLB, whereas marital status has no relationship with WLB. Based on the level of task autonomy, task variety, spouse support, parental demand, and work schedule flexibility WLB level of the employee changes significantly.
26	(Toston, 2014) QL	19 women leaders of the Church of God in Christ, U.S.	Identified prayer as one of the strategies for achieving work-life balance. Work-life balance strategies should be psychological cum physical.
27	(Chaudhari, 2013) QT	298 professionals from hospital sector Agra, India.	Respondents have a good level of WLB based on mean score (used a self-defined measure). The difference in perception of WLB based on job designation and type of hospital (public and private)
28	(Copeland, 2013) QL	12 oncology nurses from Houston Metropolitan area, U.S.A	Work-life balance is about managing time between work and home activity. Lack of time and emotional demand were the major hurdles faced by oncology nurses in achieving work-life balance. Demographics and availability

			of organisational resources influence the work-life balance. Furthermore, self-care helps to increase work-life balance level. Having work-life balance produce a positive effect at work-life as well as at the personal life of the employee.
29	(Devi, 2013) QT	500 IT employees from Chennai, TN, India.	Identified 56 variables affecting the WLB of the employee into 5 independent factors viz., organisational policy, management role, work-life conflicts, personal-family barriers, and family activities. The study further found that the mean score for WLB was 'high' on all the 5 factors.
30	(Kumari S. , 2013) QT	250 IT (women) professionals across India.	WLB has a relationship with employee performance. WLB factors such as supportive work culture and flexible work schedule influence the employee performance. According to the researcher factors affecting WLB were flexi-work conditions, supportive working environment, stress at workplace, working hours, work culture and provision for extra benefits.
31	(Komodromou, 2013) Mixed	487 working professionals from the U.K.	Providing WLB benefits helps to enhance the organisational commitment (OC) and job satisfaction among employees by enhancing their perception

			towards distributive justice and organisational support.
32	(Muthulakshmi, 2013) QT	500 women in managerial post, service sector, Tamil Nadu, India.	Identified and categorised factors affecting WLB of women employees into seven categories such as time-based factors, strain-based factors, supportive network, gender discrimination, stress related factors, dependent care and leave strategies. It has also been found that women employed in the service sector face severe work-life imbalance.
33	(Shree, 2013) QT	243 nurse (critical care) Coimbatore, TN, India.	There is work-family interference among respondents. Long work hours and night shift were the important hindrances in balancing work and family responsibilities. Spouse adaptability reduces work-family conflict. Work-family conflict has a relationship with poor physical and psychological health.
34	(Sree, 2013) QT	550 employees from Andhra Pradesh, India.	The majority (78%) of the respondents have work-life balance. Weekend work, long work hours and compulsory overtime hinder employees in achieving WLB.
35	(Swarnalatha T. , 2013) QT	600 banking professionals (women) Chennai, India.	Nationalised bank employees have better WLB as compared with private bank employees. Work policies and practices have a significant relationship with WLB.

36	(Vernon, 2013) Qualitative (QL)	30 working professionals, Canada	Factors such as work hours, workload, workspace and spill over in between domain have a relationship with work-life conflict. On the other hand, perceived meaningfulness about work as well as job satisfaction increase resilience against WLC.
37	(Bruton, 2012) QL	26 working professionals from Birmingham.	Individuals personal capability is the key element in achieving WLB. The personal capability of an individual is the result of his collegiality, contentment, commitment and control.
38	(Ervin, 2012) QL	47 athletic professionals from Georgia, U.S.A.	Job status and responsibility have no relationship with WLB level.
39	(Khan, 2012) QT	417 bank staff Madurai, TN, India	Variables such as the age, educational qualification, gender, experience, income, marital status, spouse employment status, age of the youngest child, caring responsibility and family time have an association with WLB. Similarly, the work-life imbalance has a relationship with role autonomy, role ambiguity, role conflict, and role overload.
40	(Leyden, 2012) QL	8 construction workers Ontario, Canada.	Employees have the tendency to get content (perceived powerlessness is a factor responsible) with the situation in which they are in. Hours of work doesn't have any direct relationship with WLB.

41	(Malaviya, 2012) QT	200 educational professionals, Delhi, India	The majority (61%) of the respondents face work-life imbalance. The work-life imbalance has negative implications both on the family as well as professional life on an employee. Demographic variables, individual traits, work environment, and family environment have relationship with WLB.
42	(Mukhtar, 2012) QT	143 teachers from Iowa state university, U.S.A.	There is a relationship between faculty discipline and WLB. JS and faculty discipline has no relationship. There is a relationship between JS and WLB. Demographic variables have a relationship with WLB.
43	(Mehtha, 2012) QT	263 service sector employees (woman), Pune.	Respondents identified work-life balance as very important to them. The majority (96%) of the respondent's states that they are having work-life imbalance. Personal demographics, work demographics, and family demographics have relationship with WLB.
44	(Sonia, 2012) QT	604 IT sector employees, Chennai, TN, India.	The study identified that an increase in factors such as support from supervisors, explicit work policies, progressive work culture, support from the co-worker, perfect workplace ambiance promote the WLB. Whereas an increase in factors such as work overload, complaint work culture, personal time, negative

			affectivity, implied work culture and sleep slangs results in work-life imbalance.
45	(Stepanova, 2012) QL	44 working professionals from Mutua, Barcelona.	An employee's work-life integration (balance) is influenced by organisational, inter-individual and individual factors embedded with the national context. Prevailing socio-economic conditions (availability of job), work culture (dedication towards work), organisational culture, supervisor and co-worker attitude, and individual characteristics have relationship with employee WLB.
46	(Sunderaraj, 2012) QT	400 police personals from Coimbatore City, TN, India.	Socio-economic variables such as age, gender, experience, job rank, work location, marital status, kid status, income, and education have relationship with WLB. Internal locus of control and external locus of control have relationship with WLB.
47	(Barge, 2011) QL	30 working African American women from U.S.	Flexibility is the top factor responsible for work-life balance. The absence of personal time and self-care was the top priority items that often missed by the women employee. Faith and family background were identified as a significant force that influences the work-life balance of women. Furthermore, the researcher

			also found status identity, relationship, motivation, and adaptive style as secondary theme responsible for work-life balance.
48	(Cameron, 2011) QL	30 mid-level student administrators from the U.S.A.	Time demand is identified as the most important impediment against WLB. It was followed by role multiplicity and the absence of a supportive network. The absence of organisational programmes and policies to support WLB, poor supervision and unhealthy workplace norms also act as a hindrance in achieving WLB.
49	(Jyothi, 2011) QT	443 working women from Hyderabad, India.	Employee demographics have relationship with WLB. Sociological changes such as wide spared evolvement of the nuclear family and dual-carrier job-ship act as an impediment in achieving WLB. Placing themselves at a non-transferable job is one of the most commonly applied tools to handle the problem of work-life imbalance.
50	(Simard, 2011) QL	8 employees from non-profit organisation, Canada.	Work schedule flexibility, support, and understanding (supervisor and co-worker) were the key elements for achieving WLB in life. Social support, flexibility and resource availability (at work, family and personal level) act as facilitators of WLB.

51	(Walia, 2011) QT	308 IT employees from Punjab, India.	Based on the mean score obtained on WLB scale, respondents are having 'above average' WLB level. Emotional intelligence has a positive relationship with WLB. Work centrality and spouse support have a positive relationship with WLB. Whereas household responsibility and parental demand have no relationship with WLB.
52	(Matuska, 2010) QT	458 working professionals from Minnesota, U.S.A.	Low stress, high job satisfaction level, and increased personal wellbeing have the potential to predict WLB significantly. The respondent's demographics fount to have no relationship with WLB.
53	(Mukesh, 2010) QT	640 IT professionals from Chennai, India.	Emotional intelligence, work silence and career identity silence moderates the relationship between WLB (dependent variable) and family characteristics, family resources, work characteristics, and work resources.
54	(Gurney, 2009) QL	40 employees from ResearchOrg, Scotland.	Employee psychology has a relationship with WLB. Work and family life limits the time available for leisure. Gender norms and exacerbates the work-life imbalance. Similarly, the professionals face more imbalance than that of non-professionals.

55	(Branch, 2008) QT	77 accountants from New Zealand	Identified and categorised WLB initiatives into six categories viz., leave related, work-hour related, recreation-related, work-related, work/home and study related. Work flexibility alone doesn't enhance WLB, rather employees should be made aware of WLB policies offered and the employees should be supported to use the WLB policies.
56	(Crozier-Durham, 2007) QL	12 school leaders from Victoria, Australia	The study identified three types of activities that contribute towards WLB viz., off job strategies, personal strategies and on-the-job strategies. Psychological resources, physical resources, and role flexibility contribute towards WLB.
57	(Fun, 2007) QT	112 employees from Hong Kong city, China	The turnover intention has an inverse relationship with family-friendly policies, flexi-time, five-day week, family leave policy and employee assistance programmes. Similarly, the five day work week and employee assistance programmes have a positive relationship with job satisfaction.
58	(Thomas.K, 2007) QT	350 working women across Kerala	Religious values have a relationship with family identity, Christian women gave more preference to the family. In the management of work-family conflict spouse support

			and family support have an important role in relicensing. Compared to the family domain work domain has greater conflict potential.
59	(Päivi & Andrea, 2007) QL	12 managerial employees, Sweden	WLB was primarily the responsibility of the employees themselves. Organisations and government can only act as facilitators or mediator in achieving the WLB by providing policies and facilities.
60	(Esson, 2004) QT	181 teaching professionals from Jamaica	Simple demographic clustering such as age, marital status, and tenure doesn't have any relationship with work-family conflict. Work-related variables such as work stress and workload have significant relation with work-family conflict.

References

Barge, G. C. (2011). *A Phenomenological Study of Competing Priorities and African American Women Striving to Achieve Work-Life Balance.* Ph.D Thesis.

Bauer, S. (2017). *Work-Life Balanced Culture, Work Flexibility, and Inducements: Impact on Perceived Organizational Attractiveness and Job Pursuit Intention.* Master Degree Thesis.

Branch, S. (2008). *The Effects of Organisational Work-Life Balance Initiatives on Accountants in New Zealand.* University of Canterbury . anterbury : Sarah Branch.

Bruton, A. (2012). *Work Life Balance and the Workforce Reforms.* PhD Thesis, University of Birmingham, School of Education, Birmingham.

Cameron, T. L. (2011). *The Professional & the Personal: Worklife Balance and Mid-Level Student Affairs Administrators.* Blacksburg: Tracey LaShawne Cameron.

Chaudhari, S. (2013). *A Study on the Perception of Work-Life Balance Among Healthcare Professionals.* PhD Thesis, Dayalbagh Educational Institute, Department of Management, Agra.

Cioffi, D. (2018). *College President Perceptions of Personal Wellness: Exploring "Well-ish" and the Work-Life Balance of Mid-Career Private College Presidents.* Ann Arbor: ProQuest.

Copeland, A. D. (2013). *A Qualitative Study of Clinical Oncology Nurses Perceptions of Work-Life Balance.* Ph.D Thesis, University of Phoenix.

Crozier-Durham, M. (2007). *Work/Life Balance: Personal and Organisational Strategies of School Leaders.* Master Degree Thesis, Victoria University, Victoria .

Devi, D. R. (2013). *Study of Personal Related Factors Related to Work-Life Balance on Job Satisfaction among Selected Information Technology Employees in Chennai.* PhD Thesis, Periyar University, Department of Management, Selam.

Ervin, S. M. (2012). *A Comparative Analysis of Work-Life Balance in Intercollegiate Athletic Graduate Assistants and Supervisors.* Georgia State University, Department of Kinesiology and Health. Georgia: Georgia State University. Retrieved from http://scholarworks.gsu.edu

Esson, P. L. (2004). *Consequences of Work-Family Conflict: Testing a New Model of Work-Related, Non-Work-Related and Stress-Related Outcomes.* Virginia Polytechnic Institute and State University , Psychology. Blacksburg, VA: Patrice L. Esson.

Farkiya, R. (2015). *A Study of Work Life Balance in Health Care Industry.* PhD Thesis, Indore.

Fun, C. H. (2007). *Work-Life Balance: The Impact of Family Friendly Policies on Employees' Job Satisfaction and Turnover Intention .* Hong Kong Baptist University. Hong Kong: Hong Kong Baptist University.

Gananapalli, S. (2015). *Work Life Balance of Women Employees in State Bank of India.* PhD Thesis, Sri Krishnadevaraya Institute of Management, Anantapur.

Gowgisk, N. S. (2015). *Stress and Work/Life Balance among Employees of Manufacturing and IT Sector.* PhD Thesis, Universityof Mysore, Department of Studies in Social Work, Mysore.

Gurney, S. (2009). *Gender, work-life balance and health amongst women and men in administrative, manual and technical jobs in a single organisation: a qualitative study.* University of Glasgow . Glasgow : University of Glasgow. Retrieved from http://theses.gla.ac.uk/1641/

Isdell, L. (2016). *Work-Family Balance among Mothers who are Mid-Career Student Affairs Administrators at Institutions Recognized for Work-Life Policies.* Master Degree Thesis, University of Kansas.

Jena, S. (2014). *A comparative study on work life balance of nursing staff working in private and government hospitals with special reference to selected hospitals in odisha.* PhD Thesis, KIIT University, School of Management, Bhubaneswar.

Jhamat, M. (2015). *Association of Personal Values and Work Exploration with Work Life Balance of Women Professionals of Northern India.* PhD Thesis, Lovely Professional University, Department of Studies in Education, Phagwara.

Jones, K. (2018). *Work-Life Balance: Organizational Leadership and Individual Strategies among Successful Women Real Estate Brokers.* Ph.D, Pepperdine University , Graduate School of Education and Psychology.

Jyothi, V. S. (2011). *Work-Life Balance among Women employees in Organizations: A Study in Andhra Pradesh.* PhD Thesis, University of Hyderabad, Department of Management, Hyderabad.

Kaur, R. (2014). *Work Life Balance A Study of Rail Coach Factory Kapurthala (Punjab).* PhD Thesis, Himachal Pradesh University, Department of Cpmmerce, Shimla.

Khan, S. N. (2012). *A Study on Work Life Balance (WLB) among executives at Commerical Banks at Madurai District.* PhD Thesis, Madurai Kamaraj University, Department of Commerce, Madurai.

Komodromou, J. M. (2013). *Work-life balance benefits: Employee attitudes and behaviors through the lens of social exchange theory.* Aston University. Aston: Janell Marie Bellegante Komodromou.

Kumari, S. (2013). *Work-Life Balance And Its Impact on Performance of Women Executives in IT Companies .* PhD Thesis, Himachal Pradesh University, Shimla.

Lakshmi, K. (2015). *Work Life Balance of Femael Nurses in Private Tertiary Hospitals.* SRM University, Kattankulathur.

Leyden, M. (2012). *There's No Place like Home: Perceived Powerlessness and Work-Life Balance of Male Residential Construction Workers in Southern Ontario.* University of Guelph, Department of Sociology. Guelph, Ontario: University of Guelph.

Mahajan, S. S. (2016). *A Study of Work Life Balance and its Impact on Professional Couples.* PhD Thesis, Pune.

Malaviya, V. (2012). *Determinants of Work Life Imbalance among Faculty Members of Higher Educational Institutes in Delhi.* Bhagwant University Ajmer, Department of Management, Ajmer.

Martin, L. K. (2016). *Norway Leads the World in Gender Equality and Work-Life Balance: A Qualitative Life Course Study of Norwegian Women.* Ph.D Thesis.

Matuska, K. (2010). *Validity Evidence for a Model and Measure of Life Balance.* PhD Thesis, University of Minnesota, Minnesota.

Mehtha, M. R. (2012). *A Study of Work Life Balance (WLB) among Women Employees in the Service Sector with Special Reference to Pune City.* PhD Thesis, Tilak Maharashtra Vidyapeeth, Pune.

Mirji, H. (2014). *A Study of Work life balance in Banking Sector.* PhD Thesis, Pune.

Mukesh, D. N. (2010). *Work Family Enrichment and Work Life Balance.* Anna University, Chennai.

Mukhtar, F. (2012). *Work life balance and job satisfaction among faculty at Iowa State University.* Iowa State University . Iowa: Farah Mukhtar.

Muthulakshmi, S. (2013). *Work Life Balance of Managerial Women- An Empirical Study with Reference to Tamil Nadu.* PhD Thesis, Madurai Kamaraj University, Virudhunagar.

Olund, V. L. (2016). *A Qualitative Study of Email Overload and Virtual Working Women's Self-Perceived Job-Related Stress and Work-Life Balance .* ProQuest LLC.

Päivi, K., & Andrea, N. (2007). *Work to live, don't live to work! A cross-sectional study of the work-life balance of higher managers .* Master Degree Thesis, Umea University, Sweden, Umea School of Business, Sweden.

Prassadh, V. P. (2014). *Work Life Balance of Women Employees in BPO Indistry: A Study in Tamil Nadu.* PhD Thesis, Madurai.

Rajkumar, R. (2014). *Work Life Balance of IT Professionals in Relation to their Self Consept, Hardiness, and Emotional Maturity. .* PhD Thesis, Annamalai University, Department of Business Administration, Annamalai Nagar.

Rothberg, S. (2014). *The Journey of Female Cancer Patients or Survivors while Striving for Personal Work-life Balance .* ProQuest LLC.

Sengupta, M. (2015). *A Critical Analysis of Gender Perception of Work-Life Balance in the Service Sector in Pune.* PhD Thesis, Department of Management , Jhunjhunu.

Shah, S. S. (2014). *The Role of Work-Family Enrichment in WorkLife Balance & Career Success: A Comparison of German & Indian Managers.* Munich: Shalaka Sharad Shah.

Shahisaman, L. (2015). *A Phenomenological Study of Women in India Striving to Achieve Work-Life Balance in Finance with Competing Priorities.* Ann Arbor: ProQuest.

Shree, R. M. (2013). *A Study on Worklife Balance and Life Satisfaction of Critical Care Nurses at Coimbatore District.* Bharathiar University, Coimbatore.

Simard, M. (2011). *EmployeesP erceptions of Work Life Balance.* Recreation and Leisure Studies. Waterloo: University of Waterloo.

Sonia, G. (2012). *An Empirical Study on the Patterns of the Work Life Balance among the Employees of IT Companies in Chennai.* PhD Thesis, Alagappa University, School of Management, Karaikudi.

Sree, G. K. (2013). *Work Life Balance of Employees.* Andhra University, Department of Commerce and Management Studies, Visakhapatnam.

Stepanova, O. (2012). *Work-Life Balance in Organizational Subcultures The Case of Mutua.* PhD Thesis, University of Barcelona, Barcelona.

Sunderaraj, R. (2012). *Psychometric Study on Locus of Control and its Magnitude of Influence on Stress and Work Life Balance - With reference to Non Gazetted Officers of Coimbatore City Police.* Bharathiar University, Commerce.

Susi.S. (2014). *A Study on Work-Life Balance among ITES in the Bangalore City.* PhD Thesis, Bharathiar University, Management, Coimbatore.

Swarnalatha, T. (2013). *An Empirical Analysis of work-life balance on Woman Employees: A Study with Reference to Banking Sector at Chennai.* PhD Thesis, Manonmaniam Sundaranar University, Tirunelveli.

Thomas.K, C. (2007). *Work-Life Balance - A Sociological Study of Women Professionals in Kerala.* Mahatma Gandhi University, Kottayam, Department of Sociology, St Theresa's College, Ernakulam.

Toston, S. (2014). *Work-life Balance Straegies of Women Leaders within the Church of God in Christ.* Ann Arbor: ProQuest LLC.

Triplett, J. (2016). *The Work-Life Balance of Female Adjunct Faculty at Southern California Community Colleges.* Ann Arbor: ProQuest LLC.

Ufoegbune, V. I. (2016). *A Phenomenological Study of the Work–life balance of Nigerian Women Leadership and their vision of Nigerian Education .* Ph.D Thesis.

Varghese, S. (2015). *Management of Work Life Balance in the Banking Sector.* PhD Thesis, Mumbai.

Vernon, W. A. (2013). *Factors Responsible for Work-Life Conflict: A Study Comparing the Teaching and Legal Professions.* Ontario: University of Western Ontario.

Walia, P. (2011). *Work Life Balance of Working Professionals - A Study of IT and ITES Industry.* Punjabi University, School of Management Studies, Patiala.

CHAPTER - 4

REVIEW - ARTICLE

"Philosophy used to be a field that had content, but then 'natural philosophy' became physics, and physics has only continued to make inroads. Every time there's a leap in physics, it encroaches on these areas that philosophers have carefully sequestered away to themselves, and so then you have this natural resentment on the part of philosophers"

- Lawrence M. Krauss (Physicist)

Academic journals had a very heavy past, they have been in survived for about more than 340 years (Solomon, 2007). Academic journals are widely accessible and were published much sooner than books and accorded as very important in the promotion of academic research as compared to other means of distributing research output (Thyer, 2008). It is because of these particular characteristics possessed by the medium, the academic journals got wider acceptability in the field of research as a medium for disseminating the research output across the academicians and fellow researchers. Table 4.1, presents the chronological distribution of various journal articles, newspaper reports and seminar proceedings reviewed as the part of the study. The review is arranged in this section chronologically in descending order.

Table 4.1			
Table Showing Review in Terse - Articles			
No	Study & Type	Sample	Major Finding
1	(Hirschi, Shockley, & Zacher, in press)	Conceptual paper	Developed an action based on two-dimensional strategies to achieve work-family balance. The engagement dimension includes resource allocation and resource adjustment according to the work-family goals. Similarly, the disengagement dimension includes refinement as well as the development of work-family balance goals and sequencing of work-family goals according to the environmental change.
2	(Abdullah, Aremu, & Abogunrin, 2018)QT	165 academic staff from three universities in Nigeria.	Work-life balance has a positive effect on employee performance. Similarly, the work schedule flexibility also has a positive impact on employee performance.
3	(Beha, Drobnič, Präg, Baierl, & Eckner, 2018)QT	14097 employees from 22 European countries.	Part-time employees showed a higher level of work-life balance satisfaction compared to full-time employees. Furthermore, women in the part-time managerial job have a higher level of work-life balance satisfaction in comparison with men in part-time managerial job. Supportive framework and cultural inclinations also found to have a relationship with satisfaction with work-life balance.

4	(Choa & Allen, 2018) QL	Conceptual Paper	Introduced the concept of transitional families (families at which members are geographically dispersed) and its effect on work-family balance.
5	(Kalliath, Kalliath, Chan, & Chan, 2018) QT	428 professional social workers across India.	At a higher level of family support there is a high level of work-family enrichment, job wellbeing, and job satisfaction. The relationship between work-family resources and job satisfaction is moderated by family support which is then mediated by the job wellbeing.
6	(Kurowska, 2018) QT	1855 and 974 respondents from Poland and Sweden respectively.	In the case of high egalitarian communities, the negative effect of home-based work affects both genders equally. Whereas, in the case of low egalitarian communities, the negative effect of home-based work affects women only.
7	(Li, 2018) QT	363 employees from state owned enterprises in China.	Work-life balance has a positive relationship with organisational commitment. Similarly, the work-life balance can contribute to positive organisational outcomes. Furthermore, work-life balance has a relationship with demographic and organisational factors.
8	(Owens, Kottwitz, Tiedt, & Ramirez, 2018)	Literature review	Strategies such as self-mentoring, self-care, promotion of physical health, socialising and cognitive

			approach can help to manage work-life imbalance by reducing stress.
9	(Prithi & Vasumathi, 2018) QT	500 women employed in tannery industry, Tamil Nadu, India.	Work-life balance has a relationship with hours of work. Out of various employee related demographics considered, current experience and dual-earner status were the most important predictors of employee stress. Supervisors and/colleagues support, work schedule flexibility and time off during school holidays were the most preferred work-life balance interventions that employee like to have.
10	(Simonea, Agusa, Lasioa, & Serria, 2018) QT	707 employed personals from Italy.	Developed and validated (internal and concurrent) a 14 itemised for dimensional Italian measure of work-family interference.
11	(Zakaria, Mat, & Abdullah, 2018) QT	340 teaching staff from Malaysia.	Extraversion and conscientiousness have a positive relationship with work-life balance
12	(Bansal & Raj, 2017) QT	35 women staff from IOC LTD. Mathura, India	Fount that the WLB is independent of work-related demographics as well as personal related demographics of the respondents.
13	(Casper, Vaziri, Wayne, DeHauw, & Greenhaus, 2017) QL	Grounded theory	Identified that the jingle-jangle fallacy often rides the WLB research. Furthermore, the researchers defined WLB as a psychological process that inculcates the effect of satisfaction, fit, effectiveness

			and involvement between work and non-work activities.
14	(Ayudhya, Prouska, & Beauregard, 2017) QL	20 Greek professionals	Work-life balance and quality of life is the function of capability (individual, institutional and societal) and entitlement.
15	(Cholasseri & Senthilkumar, 2017) QT	50 college faculty from Malappuram, Kerala, India	The respondents (teaching faculty) were satisfied with the WLB. The study defines WLB as a dynamic and multi-dimensional construct which is a blend of job security, adequate salary, allowance, social status, promotion, superior-subordinate relationship, student matters, career development programmes, and other facilities.
16	(Dhanya & Kinslin, 2017) QT	100 women staff from ULCCS LTD. Kerala, India.	Respondents are having satisfactory WLB level. WLB have a relationship with experience, hours of work, education, marital status, relationship with the co-worker and organisational culture.
17	(Dhanya.S & Ravi, 2017) QT	350 women faculty from professional colleges in Kerala, India	The women faculty have moderate WLB level based on the means score obtained on the WLB scale. Individual strategies were very common among women faculty members to cope up with the work-life. Maid support and compression of hobbies and physical fitness were the most popular

			individual oriented strategies adopted.
18	(Ganiyu, Fields, & Atiku, 2017) QT	269 employees from two manufacturing firms, Lagos Metropolis, Nigeria	With the help of correlation analysis, it is found that the work-life balance strategies (WLBS) has a relationship with family satisfaction (FS) and work satisfaction (WS). Furthermore, work-life balance strategies together with work-family satisfaction can predict employee job performance significantly.
19	(Mugeanyi, 2017) QL	Conceptual review, Canada	Self-awareness is the key to WLB. In order to have the balance between work and life, one should be aware of the self. Self-awareness enables an individual to understand his emotions and provide self-care.
20	(Otusile, Ibeh, & Ndubuisi, 2017) QT	Literature review on work-life balance	Work-life balance can instil an individual a sense of fulfilment. Work-life balance is about having proper management of time between work and non-work activities and having a proper mind-set to set goals for various life domains effectively.
21	(Suresh & Kodikal, 2017) QT	214 nursing staff from multispecialty hospitals, Mangalore, India	Work to family conflict (79.4% of the respondents faces work to family conflict) is very significant among the nursing staff. Work to family conflict (WFC) mediates the relationship between work-related factors and JS. Furthermore, WFC also

			mediates the relationship between work-related factors and turnover intention.
22	(Tambe, 2017) QL	Literature review India	WLB is a construct which is gender neutral in nature. However, traditionally WLB is addressed as a feminine subject. WLB is essential for every employee and it helps to enhance employee productivity, performance, and employee retention.
23	(Abe, Fields, & Abe, 2016) Mixed	Government servants of South Africa. Interview -11 staff Survey - 307 staff	There's a relationship between employee wellness programmes and WLB. Employee wellness programmes are not work-life balance strategies as work-life balance strategies can predict only 7.1% change in employee wellness.
24	(Dhanya.J.S & Kinslin.D, 2016) QT	318 women faculty from engineering colleges, Kerala, India	Based on the mean score obtained on WLB scale there is a moderate level of WLB. Sector of employment has a relationship with WLB.
25	(Direnzo, Greenhaus, & Weer, 2016) QT	367 workers from U.S employed fulltime.	Identified that there is a positive relationship between Protean Career Orientation (PCO) and WLB. Availability of resources (work-life balance policies, support programmes.,) doesn't guarantee. Whereas the ability of the employee to make use of resources enable them to strike balance between work and non-work.

26	(Greubel, Arlinghaus, Nachreiner, & Lombardi, 2016) QT	Two studies in the year 2005 (N = 23934) and 2010 (N = 35187) with employees from 27 E.U. nations.	Abnormal work shift (weekend work/shift and evening work) is associated with the lower work-life balance and increased health complaints among the employees.
27	(Jindal, 2016) QT	100 women who are employed in the service sector from Chandigarh and Mohali, Punjab, India	Earning level of the women have a significant relationship with their WLB level. That is, there's a positive relationship between earning and WLB. Similarly, WLB has a relationship with the quality of work life.
28	(Lakshmipriya & Krishna, 2016) QT	152 women entrepreneurs from South Bengaluru, India.	The positive family-work spillover has a relationship with spouse support and family support. Furthermore, there is a positive relationship between positive family-work spillover and employee work-life balance.
29	(Padmanabhan & Kumar, 2016) QT	70 women employees from information and communication technology firms Bengaluru, India	High level of WLC is associated with low level of WLB. WLC occurs when the support system is unable to absorb the difference in between work and family roles.
30	(Pradhan, Jena, & Kumari, 2016) QT	206 manufacturing employees from public sector undertakings, India	Organisational Citizenship Behaviour (OCB) has relationship with WLB. Furthermore, the OCB mediate the relationship

			between WLB and Organisational Commitment.
31	(Sudha.D, Anitha.S, & Harikumar, 2016) QT	150 Women Gynaecologists from Kerala, India	Developed a ten-item three factorised scale to measure the Job Related Issues (JRI) faced by the women doctors leading to WLB. High level of JRI has an association with a high level of workplace support issues, a high level of self-esteem issues and a high level of working situation issues.
32	(Szener, Grzankowski, Eng, Odunsi, & Frederick, 2016) QT	72 Gynaecologists and Oncologists from the U.S.A.	Only the minority (22%) of the respondents were satisfied with the present level of work-life balance satisfaction. Respondents age, level of fatigue and hours of work have a relationship with work-life balance satisfaction. However, marital status, parental status, and gender doesn't fount any association with work-life balance satisfaction. Furthermore, the researchers also need to explore the relationship between workforce impact and the absence of work-life balance.
33	(Smeltzer, et al., 2016) QT	554 doctoral program faculty from the U. S.	Validated the enrichment cum interference model of WLB, proposed by Gwenith G. Fisher in the year 2001. (i.e., WLB = work interference with personal-life (WIPL) + personal-life interference with work (PLIW) + work and

			personal-life enrichment (WPLE).
34	(Toffoletti & Starr, 2016) QL	Interviewed 31 women faculty from an Australian university.	WLB is the responsibility of the employee rather than the responsibility of the employer. Disclosure of the WLB policy has a positive association with employee WLB level. The mental perception of the employee about the work itself has an impact on their ability to balance work and non-work activities.
35	(Zakaria & Omar, 2016) QT	102 bank employees from Malaysia.	Transformational leadership style has as association with employee WLB level. However, the demographic characteristics of the employee such as age, gender, and marital status were independent of WLB.
36	(Antai, Oke, Braithwaite, & Anthony, 2015) QT	4186 working people from Denmark, Norway, Finland, and Sweden.	Poor work-life balance was associated with self-reported sickness absence and increased health problems.
37	(Banu, A, 2015)	387 IT employees from Chennai, India	Respondents experience Work Interference with Personal Life (WIPL) often than that of Personal Life Interference with Work (PLIW). There is a direct positive relationship between satisfaction with WLB and improved effectiveness at work.
38	(Brough, Siu, O'Driscoll, &	234 respondents	Both the Work to Family Enrichment (WFE) and the

	Timmis, 2015) QT	from Australian Organisations.	Family to Work Enrichment (FWE) have a positive relationship with self-efficiency. Furthermore, self-efficiency has a positive relationship with work-life balance. Similarly, the work-life balance has a positive relationship with family satisfaction and work satisfaction.
39	(Eraranta, 2015) QL	Conceptual study.	Work-life balance is the management philanthropy evolved as a result of social scientific knowledge. Wide spared acceptance of humanitarian values transformed the corporate management philanthropy and it has become a common law that the employment opportunities should be opened up for everyone in the society equally.
40	(Kumari & Selvi, 2015) QT	Employees from Ericsson company, Chennai, India	WLB is an important concern for employees themselves. WLB have not much impact on JS.
41	(Monica.M, 2015) QT	100 employees from State Bank of Mysore, India	Employees of the State Bank of Mysore are able to balance the work and life. Social needs have a positive relationship with personal needs, time management, teamwork, compensation benefits, and work itself.
42	(Orkibi & Brandta, 2015) QT	108 employees from advertising and	The employee ability to manage work-life balance fully mediate the relationship

		accounting firms, Israel	between positive orientation and job satisfaction. That is, the positive psychology of the employee can facilitate WLB and JS.
43	(Rao, 2015) QT	100 employees from 4 different companies in Visakhapatnam, India	Personal factors and demographic factors of the employee have a relationship with WLB. Work-life satisfaction of the employee can be enhanced by providing opportunities for teamwork, work schedule flexibility and developing a family-friendly work culture.
44	(Raj & Julius, 2015) QT	184 fathers from Hyundai Motors, India.	Support from the family is the core factor responsible for work-life balance. Furthermore, the year of experience and organisational interventions have no effect on employee work-life balance.
45	(Renthlei & Singh, 2015) QT	200 teaching faculty (private school) from Mizoram, India	The demographic characteristics pertaining to the employee such as gender, income, marital status, and experience have no relationship WLB level.
46	(Sharma & Nair, 2015) QL	Conceptual study	Defined work-life balance as the ability of the employee to manage stress and time between various life domains.
47	(Swarnalatha & Rajalakshmi, 2015) QT	241 educational professionals from private and public colleges T.N, India.	Work-life balance has an association with JS and organisational commitment. Similarly, the organisational initiatives have a relationship with WLB level of the

			employee. Whereas the turnover intention doesn't have any relationship with WLB.
48	(Timmis, Brough, Siu, O'Driscoll, & Kalliath, 2015) QT	International and cross cultural study with a sample of 6983 employees from Australia and New Zealand; 3871 employees from china; 567 employees from Hong Kong	Validated the Brough et al., 2014 scale of WLB. Longitudinal as well as cross-sectional validity of the scale has been established. Work-life balance is a construct which is subjective in nature and therefore, the local themes and sentiments have an influence on employee work-life balance concept.
49	(Azeem & Akhtar, 2014) QT	275 employees from public and private hospitals, Uttar Pradesh (U.P), India.	There is a moderate level of WLB, JS and organisational commitment among the respondents. Both job satisfaction, as well as organisational commitment, have a significant relationship with WLB. JS together with organisational commitment accounts for 37 % of the variance in WLB.
50	(Banu & Duraipandian, 2014) QT	387 IT professionals from Chennai, India.	Five-dimensional 46 item scale has been developed with the help of factor analysis for the measurement of WLB of the IT professionals. According to the study work-life balance of an employee is influenced by five factors viz., workplace support, work interference with personal life, personal life interference

			with work, satisfaction with work-life balance and improved effectiveness at work.
51	(Brough, et al., 2014) QT	6983 employees from Australia and New Zealand	In accordance with the WLB definition proposed by Kalliath & Brough, 2008 developed a new unidimensional four itemised scale to measure employee WLB level. The scale fount valid both cross-sectionally as well as longitudinally.
52	(Haslam, Filus, Morawska, Sanders, & Fletcher, 2014) QT	569 working (either part time or full time) parents from Australia.	A new scale has been developed for the measurement of WFC and FWC. The scale has got 10 items, 5 items each measuring the level of WFC level and FWC level.
53	(Kacmar, Crawford, Carlson, Ferguson, & Whitten, 2014) QT	639 working people. U.S – collection outsourced- online medium.	Shortened the work-family enrichment scale of Carlson, Kacmar, Wayne, and Grzywacz in 2006 into a six itemised two-dimensional scale. The scale found valid in terms of discriminant validity, convergent validity and predictive validity wise.
54	(Lavassani & Movahedi, 2014) QL	Review about theories and measures of WLB, U.S.A.	Work-life balance studies can be broadly classified into three categories viz., conflict based studies, compensation based studies (i.e., conflict plus enrichment) and balance based studies.
55	(Lyness & Judiesch, 2014) QT	40921 managers from 36 countries	Supervisors perception of employees WLB varies by ratee gender and nationality.

			Egalitarian values found to have a significant association with employee WLB. In the case of low egalitarian nations women have low WLB in comparison with men. Whereas in the case of high egalitarian nations, women have similar WLB level in comparison with men.
56	(Morganson, Litano, & O'Neill, 2014) QL	Qualitative and conceptual study based on literature	WFB has an association with positive psychology. That is, cognitive strengths and psychological resources were related to WFB. Furthermore, the leadership style also has an association with employee WLB. Appreciative inquiry, cognitive training, and psychological motivation offered as the part of formal intervention strategy promote WLB.
57	(Muthukumar, Savitha, & Kannadas, 2014) QL	Literature review intended to identify the importance of WLB, India	WLB is the function of time management plus stress management. WLB helps in attaining equilibrium between work and non-work activities and thereby reduce the friction between work and non-work activities. WLB helps to enhance efficiency, productivity, and satisfaction.
58	(Poulose & Sudarsan.N, 2014) QL	Conceptual review on WLB, Kerala, India	Categorised factors responsible for WLB into three viz., factors relating to the personal life of the employee, factors relating to the organisational life of the

			employee and factors relating to the social life of the employee.
59	(Singh S. , 2014) QT	228 service sector employees from Northern states of India.	Developed a 24 item four-dimensional scale to measure WLB developed a new scale to measure the employee work-life balance level. The scale has got 24 items in the four different dimensions viz., positive work to family spillover, positive family to work spillover, negative work to family spillover and negative family to work spillover.
60	(Sinha, 2014) QT	100 employees of CCIL India LTD, U.P, India	Employees of CCIL India have moderate to good level of work-life balance. CCIL employees have a good quality of work-life.
61	(Sundaresan, 2014) QT	116 employed women from Bangalore City, India.	Women are having difficulty in balancing work and family life. Excessive work pressure, too little time for themselves and the need to fulfil other expectations were identified as the major cause of WLB. Whereas the consequences of poor WLB were dis-stress, anxiety, disharmony at home, job burnout and inability to rise up to the full potential.
62	(Atheya & Arora, 2013) QL	A review of literature on WLB, India	Work stress is the major cause of poor work-life balance in the case of bank employees.
63	(Chandarasekar, S, Nair, &	305 employees from Techno park,	Work-life imbalance occurs when the work demand interferes with personal life

	Ansu.S.R, 2013) QT	Trivandrum, India.	demand. WLB has a relationship with employee gender and job status. Similarly, WLB has a positive relationship with JS. Demographics such as gender, level of management and nature of job have a significant relationship with WLB.
64	(Ghanbaria, Ramazanib, & Jaliliniac, 2013) QT	205 accountants from Iran.	Work-life balance importance is dependent on employee gender.
65	(Kaur, 2013) QT	75 teaching faculty from Chandigarh, Punjab, India	WLB has an association with the personality dimensions of the employees. Similarly, WLB also has a strong positive correlation with life satisfaction.
66	(Kar & Misra, 2013) QT	100 IT sector employees from Bengaluru, India	WLB practices such as flexi-timing, career break options, employee assistance programme, child care provisions, social family events, and flexible working environment have an impact on employee retention and organisational performance.
67	(Mazerolle & Goodman, 2013) QL	Eight athletic trainers from NCAA, NC, the U.S.	Family oriented work environment, organisational support, and individual coping strategies were the important elements responsible for WLB. Identification of the self and self-care is the key to WLB.

68	(McNamaraa, Pitt-Catsouphesa, Matz-Costaa, Brownb, & Valcourc, 2013)QT	1879 respondents from the U.S.A.	Hours of work has a negative relationship with satisfaction with work-life balance. Whereas perceived work schedule fit and family supportive work culture has a positive relationship with satisfaction with work-life balance.
69	(Meenakshi & Bhuvaneshwari, 2013) QT	66 employees from BPO sector, Bengaluru, India.	BPO companies offer a wide range of WLB policies and programmes in comparison with other service sector firms. However, the existing WLB policies and programmes were not sufficient and the employees are having a work-life imbalance.
70	(Meenakshi, Subrahmanyam, & Ravichandran, 2013) QL	Study to understand the importance of WLB	WLB is about doing the work and family activities with enthusiasm and happiness.
71	(Pandu, Balu, & Poorani, 2013) QT	160 IT & ITeS employees (Married women) Chennai, India	Work environment has no association with WLB. Feelings about the work, family dependents, and absence from work have a significant association with WLB.
72	(Raj.R, 2013) QT	100 personals from pharmaceutical sector (marketing), Kerala, India	Based on the mean score obtained on WLB scale pharma marketing employees face work-life imbalance.

73	(Sheokand & Priyanka, 2013) QL	The study was conceptual in nature., India	Time management is the key to WLB. WLB is a theme influenced by technological, socio-cultural, economic and institutional factors. Demographic characteristics (work, family, personal) moderates the relationship between influencers of WLB and work-family conflict.
74	(Shiva, 2013) QT	200 working women from Kerala, India	Working women are having work-family conflict and absence of organisational satisfaction.
75	(Singh S. , 2013) QT	Literature review on WLB, India.	WLB policies and practices have a relationship with JS, work stress, career growth, turnover, absenteeism, appreciation and competitive environment.
76	(Umene-Nakano, et al., 2013) QT	704 psychiatrists from Japan.	About half (46%) of the respondent's experience difficulty in balance work and personal life. Higher level of emotional exhaustion and low level of support have significant association with low WLB.
77	(Vijayalakshmi & Latha, 2013) QT	40 teaching faculty, T.N, India	WLB has an association with respondents age and designation. Whereas, experience doesn't have any association with WLB.
78	(Viswanathan & Jeyakumaran, 2013) QT	35 (ITeS) employees Chennai. India.	Developed and validated (face and content) an 18 item five-dimensional scale for the purposes of studying WLB of the employees.

79	(Yadav & Dabhade, 2013) QT	100 women employees from SBI, M.P, India	Respondents have an average work-life balance and happy with their existing work arrangements. Likewise, WLB has an association with JS. There's ineffective work-life balance policy communication. There exists inadequacy of work-life balance policies.
80	(Ajay K.R & Amanjot, 2012) QT	100 educational professionals from Delhi, India	Conflict, enrichment, and spirituality have an influence on both WLB and subjective wellbeing. Demographics of the employee doesn't have any association with WLB. Whereas, there's a positive association between WLB and job satisfaction.
81	(Amber, Hassan, Anam, & Asif, 2012) QL	Conceptual paper	WLB is important for employees as it enhances the motivation level, satisfaction, empowerment, and commitment. Similarly, WLB is important for the organisation as it enhances the productivity, efficiency, competitiveness, and morale of the employees and thereby helps to earn a competitive advantage.
82	(Bharathy, 2012) QT	300 BPO employees from Chennai and Pondicherry, India	Respondents age have an association with the level of stress. BPO employees are facing health issues such as digestive disorders, headaches and back pain in common.

83	(Bell, Rajendran, & Theiler, 2012) QT	139 teaching faculty from Australia	Perceived job stress has an association with poor work-life balance and work-life conflict. Perceived job thread has a stronger influence on WLB and WLC than the influence of perceived job pressure stress. The employee wellbeing has a positive association with WLB. Whereas, the employee ill-being has negative association with WLB.
84	(Chandra, 2012) Mixed	Conducted 100 (50 Indian and 50 Western) semi-structured interview with HR managers of multinational companies.	In Asian nations gender, socialisation has an association with perception towards WLB. With regard to WLB American and European companies are well ahead as they give more importance to WLB and flexible working practices. Whereas, Indian companies more concentrate on employee welfare rather than flexibility.
85	(Chitra Devi & Sheela Rani, 2012)QT	280 women employees from BPO sector, Chennai, India.	There is a positive relationship between WLB, family satisfaction and life satisfaction.
86	(Fatima & A.Sahibzada, 2012) QT	146 teaching staff from various universities of Pakistan	Partner support, colleagues support, and job resources have a positive association with WLB. Whereas unfair criticism has a negative association with WLB. Gender moderates the relationship between family-related variables and WLB;

			also between work-related variables and WLB.
87	(Jayakar & Babu, 2012) QT	300 managerial staff employed with IT sector, Hyderabad, India.	Direct face to face communication has the potential to improve the work-life balance level of employee.
88	(Lakshmi, Ramachandran, & Boohene, 2012) QT	200 nursing staff (female) from Chennai, India	Majority of the women are struggling to achieve work-life balance. Sector of employment doesn't have any association with WLB.
89	(Parida, 2012) QT	162 ITes employees from Bhubaneswar, Pune, and Bangalore, India.	WLB has two dimensions the employer dimension (i.e., the things that the employee does for the employee for attaining WLB) and the employee dimension (i.e., the things that the employee does for himself for attaining the WLB)
90	(Raju, 2012) QL	WLB review, Eritrea.	Reduced turnover, job satisfaction, improved performance, better physical and mental health were the benefits of WLB
91	(Raj.R & Ramanathan, A, 2012) QT	116 paramedical staff from private hospitals, Kerala, India	WLB of the paramedical employee is good based on the mean score obtained on WLB scale (the WLB was measure with the help of Hymans (2005) scale of work-life balance).
92	(Shanafelt, et al., 2012) QT	27276 physicians from the U.S.A.	There is an association between the level of burnout and work-life balance dissatisfaction.

93	(Vanishree, 2012)QT	200 BPO employees from Hyderabad, India.	Employees are having difficulty in balancing their life among family, personal and work domains.
94	(Leaptrott & McDonald, 2011) QT	109 participants from executive training programme, South eastern the U.S.A.	Employee benefit, work environment, flexi-time, and discrimination have a relationship with job satisfaction.
95	(Mathew & Panchanatham, 2011) Mixed	Women entrepreneurs from South India, Interview (N = 26) Survey (N = 227)	Developed a five-dimensional 39 itemised scale to measure WLB. The dimensions of the scale were viz., role overload, quality of health, dependent care, time management, and support network.
96	(Patwa, 2011)QT	110 service sector employees from Insurance and Banking sector, Jaipur, India	There is a relationship between the sector of employment and WLB. Compared to the insurance sector banking sector employees have high WLB level.
97	(Rania, Kamalanabhan, & Selvarania, 2011) QT	210 IT sector employees, TN, India.	WLB has the ability to predict the JS of the employee significantly.
98	(Ratna, Gupta, Devani, & Chawla, 2011) QT	180 BPO employees from Delhi, India	Work-life balance policies were not formalised in organisations and the employees were unaware of the WLB policies and programmes in operation.
99	(Ravikumar, 2011) QT	259 BPO/ITeS employees, India.	Majority of the respondents are having health-related

			problems such as headaches and digestive disorders.
100	(Talukder, 2011) QT	50 employees from MetLife Alico, Dhaka, Bangladesh	Factors such as employee benefit, workload, flexitime, discrimination and work environment determine the WLB level of the employee.
101	(Thakur & Surampudi, 2011) QL	Interviewed 30 IT professionals from Hyderabad, India.	Identified poor time management as the key factor responsible for work-life imbalance.
102	(Doble & Supriya, 2010) QT	110 IT sector employees, TN, India	Employees strongly believe that the flexible working hours, work from home option and child care facilities at the organisational premise will enhance the WLB level. Furthermore, supportive work culture is helpful in achieving WLB.
103	(Lazar, Osoian, & Ratiu, 2010) QL	Literature review intends to identify the relation between WLB practice and organisational performance, Rumania	The work-life conflict has a significant cost attached to it in terms of poor employee engagement, absenteeism, turnover, low productivity, and poor employee retention. Work-life balance policies help the organisation to assist the employees in overcoming the issue of WLC. Work-life balance policies and programmes have the ability to enhance employee productivity, reduce turnover, enhance creativity, reduced ill-being and improved organisational image.

104	(Malik, Zaheer, Khan, & Ahmed, 2010) QT	175 medical personals (doctors) from Pakistan	WLB has no association either with the turnover intention or with job satisfaction. Whereas, WLC has a relationship with turnover intention and job satisfaction.
105	(Naithani, 2010) QL	Literature review	Factors affecting WLB can be categorised into three viz., work-related factors, personal related factors and other factors relating to the general environment. The benefits of the WLB is two dimensional in nature, employer-oriented benefits, and employee oriented benefits.
106	(Parker & Citera, 2010)QT	543 respondents from the U.S.A.	Employees who belong to the generation 'X' and the Millennials make use of WLB policies more often and widely as compared to the Baby Boomers. Similarly, there's a gender divide with regard to WLB policy usage. That is, women were making use of work-life policy more often than that of men.
107	(Reddy, Vranda, Ahmed, Nirmala, & Siddaramu, 2010) QT	90 married women from Delhi, India	Respondents are facing work to family conflict more often than family to work conflict. WLB have an association with spouse expectation, education, nature of work, the age of children and reason for working.
108	(Rincy & Panchanatham, 2010) QT	375 service sector	A four-dimensional 42 itemised scale has been developed for the purpose of

		employees from India	measuring WLB. WLB is the sum total of work-life conflict and work-life enrichment.
109	(Sakthivel & Jayakrishnan, 2010) QT	328 nurses from Cuddalure district, TN, India	Work-life balance has an association with organisational commitment. WLB = (Self-perception + WIFL + FIWL)
110	(Waumsley, Houston, & Marks, 2010) QT	940 working women from the U.K.	Developed and validated a new two dimensional ten itemised conflict/interference model based scale to measure the WLB level of the working women. WLB is a situation at which the employee experience low/minimal level of interference between work and personal life domain.
111	(Carlson, Grzywacz, & Zivnuska, 2009)QT	685 employees from the U.S.A.	Developed and validated a six itemised unidimensional scale to measure work-family balance.
112	(Emslie & Hunt, 2009) QL	21 employed personals from Scotland	Work-life balance theories and policies are gender discriminative in nature. There's an association between gender and WLB perception.
113	(Fisher, Bulger, & Smith, 2009) Mixed	Study 1 = 12 Study 2 = 540 Study 3 = 384 Sample was drawn from employed people residing in the U.S.	A 17 itemised four-dimensional scale has been developed and validated for the purpose of measuring WLB. The scale has been developed based on the interference cum enhancement model of WLB. The study pointed out the need for broadening the scope of the non-work spear by

			including non-work activities outside the scope of family. Similarly, there's a need to understand the effect of specific activities on WLB. The effect of individual differences and their impact on WLB also need to be identified.
114	(Otis, 2009) Mixed	Working women from the U.S.A. (N = 104; Interview – 10; Survey – 94)	Social support is an important assistive element in attaining WLB. In comparison with stay-in-home mom and women who were employed on a full-time basis, moms who work on part-time have the lowest level of WLB.
115	(Sharma & Mehta, 2009) QT	80 medical representatives from the city of Bhopal, India.	WLB has a significant impact on the nature of the overall sales performance of the employee.
116	(Albertsen, Rafnsdóttir, Grimsmo, Tómasson, & Kauppinen, 2008) QL	Review of WLB in light of its relation with work hours.	Based on employee gender there is a difference in the relationship between hours of work and WLB. Overtime and unstandardised work environment have a negative influence on WLB. Employee influence over work hours has a positive influence on WLB. Because of the methodical framework of WLB studies, cause and effect relationship can't be established.
117	(Gatrell & Cooper, 2008) QL	Literature review	WLB is a societal concept and the society exerts pressure on working parents to behave as a good social citizen. Change

			in the organisational culture to accommodate work flexibility and WLB.
118	(Hilla, et al., 2008)QL	Literature review focused of workplace flexibility.	Workplace flexibility should be practiced through mutual trust and respect between the employer and employee. The supportive work culture and work flexibility together with control over work schedule enhance work-life fit.
119	(Kalliath & Brough, 2008) QL	Grounded theory	Classified work-life balance studies into six heads based on the underlying theme and defined WLB as the individual perception that work and non-work activities are compactable and promote growth in accordance with an individual's current work life priorities.
120	(McMillan, Morris, & Atchley, 2008) QL	Theoretical study intended to explore the importance of WLB.	Conflict and enrichment research needs to extend beyond the individual level. Similarly, conflict, enrichment, and balance were independent constructs which are dependent on each other.
121	(Poelmans, Kalliath, & Brough, 2008) QL	Conceptual review	WLB is a concept which has a very strong association with the cognitive skill of an individual. Feminisation and greying population tends to have an influence on WLB. The content scope and with of WLB concept needs to be refined.

122	(Beauregard & Henry, 2007) QL	Literature review intends to explore the relationship between WLB and organisational policies.	Empirical studies failed to provide an exclusive conclusion that work-life balance policies enhance employee performance by reducing work-life conflict. Factors such as managerial support, job status, nationality, and cultural sentiments can act as potential mediators/moderators in the relationship between work-life balance and employee performance. WLB can be a potential facilitator to enhance organisational performance, increased cost saving, reduced employee attrition, and productivity enhancement.
123	(Bulger, Matthews, & Hoffman, 2007) QT	332 employed personals from the U.S.A.	Boundary management practice has an association with work-personal life interference and work-personal life enhancement. Low level of flexibility together with high permeability increase the work-life interference. Whereas, a high level of flexibility together with low permeability increase the work-life enhancement.
124	(Grzywacz & Carlson, 2007)QL	Grounded theory	Theoretically/conceptually defined and validated that the balance is a concept which is independent from enrichment and conflict.

125	(Haar & Bardoel, 2007) QT	420 respondents employed across Australia	Work to family/family to work negative spillover have a positive association with psychological distress and turnover intentions. Whereas positive work to family spillover has a positive association with family satisfaction.
126	(Keeton, Fenner, Johnson, & Hayward, 2007) QT	935 randomly selected physicians from the U.S.A.	Control over work hours and hours of work were the strongest predators of WLB. Age, gender, and department of work has no association with WLB. Based on means score obtained on WLB scale physicians are having moderate WLB level.
127	(Lewis, Gambles, & Rapoport, 2007) QL	A review about WLB.	WLB is a concept which is evolved from the concept of WFB. The socio-cultural refinement and turning happened in the 20th century nessiciated the development of WLB concept.
128	(Rennar, 2007) QL	Conceptual review	Work-life balance is the explanation about the magnitude of integration between work and non-work activities by an employee. It is the ability of an employee to have a healthy and recreative life both inside the organisation as well as outside the organisation.
129	(Smith & Gardner, 2007) QT	153 employees from a government	Factors such as awareness about the policy, supervisor support, work to family conflict, time demand, age,

		department New Zealand	and career damage have a relationship with the use of WLB policies. Whereas factors such as co-worker support, dependent status, family to work conflict, year of experience and organisational commitment have no relationship with WLB policies.
130	(Valcour, 2007) QT	570 call centre employees from the U.S.A.	Hours of work has a negative relationship with WLB. Job complexity and control over work time have a positive relationship with WLB satisfaction. When the hours of work rose workers with low control experience a decline in WLB satisfaction. Whereas, workers with high control did have any decline in WLB satisfaction.
131	(Carlson, Kacmar, Wayne, & Grzywacz, 2006) QT	84 employees from various organisations in U.S.A	An 18 itemised three-dimensional scale has been developed for measuring the positive side of the work-family interface (i.e., work-family enrichment).
132	(Fleetwood, 2006) QL	Descriptive paper based on literature review	Work-flexibility can be either employer-friendly or employee-friendly. The employer-friendly work flexibility constraint the employee WLB. Whereas, the employee-friendly work-flexibility enhance the WLB. The WLB is the initiative and the by-product of wide spared acceptance of neoliberalism.

133	(Greenhaus & Powell, 2006) QL	Grounded theory	Defines "work-family enrichment as the experience to which experience in one role improves the quality of life in another role".
134	(Powell & Greenhaus, 2006) QL	Concept evaluation	Found that work-family enrichment and work-family conflict were either unrelated or inversely related to each other. The resource level might have an influence on the relationship between work-family enrichment and work-family conflict, which is to be explored further.
135	(Coughlan, 2005) QT	87 employees from National University of Ireland, Maynooth, Ireland	The majority (66%) of the respondents haven't availed any kind of WLB policies. Furthermore, WLB policies were mostly picked up by women employees. Unawareness of the WLB policy was the major hindrance against using WLB policy, followed by experienced difficulty with regard to assessing initiatives and unavailability of WLB policies matching the employee needs. Flexitime, parental leave, and job sharing were the most frequently availed WLB policies.
136	(Hayman, 2005) QT	61 university staff from western Australia	Redefined the WLB scale developed by Fisher et al., 2003 scale of WLB. The redefined scale has got 15 items in three dimensions viz.,

			personal life intervention with work - 4 items, work intervention with personal life - 7 items and work/personal life enrichment - 4 items.
137	(Voydanoff, 2005) QT	1816 banking sector employees from Contiguous, U.S.	Work to family conflict and work to family facilitation partially social integration and job stress. Similarly, family to work conflict and family to work facilitation partially mediate the relationship between effective community resources and marital satisfaction and risk.
138	(Fisher & Layte, 2004)QT	150000 diaries were examined from 80000 diarists from 19 different countries.	Nationality has a relationship with the availability of free time and hours of work. Informal work environment have an association with gender role divide.
139	(Sturges & Guest, 2004) Mixed	320 Graduate workers from five large organisations in U.K.	The organisational policy regarding work and non-work have relationship with WLB. long work hours' act as a demotivation only for employees who are having low work-life balance level. furthermore, WLB has relationship with lifestyle and cultural inclination.
140	(Fisher-McAuley, Stanton, Jolton, & Gavin, 2003) QT	603 fitness professionals from the U.S. and Canada, and 545 managers from the U.S.	WLB can predict employee job strain and job satisfaction significantly. Work-life imbalance leads to occupational stress, job dissatisfaction and employee turnover.

141	(Greenhaus, Collins, & Shaw, 2003) QT	428 randomly selected members of American Institute of Certified Public Accountants.	The relationship between work-family balance and quality of life is conditional in nature. Compared to balancers, imbalancers produce only a negligible difference in engagement or satisfaction. Negative role balance can be the cause for the absence of difference between balancers and imbalancers.
142	(Grzywacz & Bass, 2003) Mixed	1986 respondents from National Survey of Midlife Development, U.S.	The work-family conflict and work-family facilitation are independent constructs. The effect of work-family conflict and work-family facilitation need to be considered separately. The mental health will be optimised when family to work facilitation is high and work to family and family to work conflict is low.
143	(Lockwood, 2003) QL	Review about the etymology of WLB	Global competition, personal lives/family values and aging workforce act as a hindrance against WLB.
144	(Villiers & Kotze, 2003) QL	20 employees were interviewed from a multinational petroleum extraction company, South Africa	Work-place issues, a managerial change, leadership pattern, supervisory support, cultural difference, and technical competence were the major factors that influence work-life conflict. WLB is an individualistic issue which is dynamic in nature. Individual oriented strategies and skills are very effective in tracking WLB in

			comparison with organisational level strategies.
145	(White, Hill, McGovern, Mills, & Smeaton, 2003) Mixed method	3389 employees from England.	There's conflict between high-performance practices (appraisal system, performance-based pay, group working practices) and work-life balance policies.
146	(Felstead, Jewson, Phizacklea, & Walters, 2002) QT	28240 employees from the U.K.	WLB is a phenomenon which is gender neutral in nature. Family friendly work atmosphere enhances the WLB level of the employees, which in turn enhance the employee performance.
147	(Guest, 2002) QL	Review about the perspectives of WLB.	The existing conceptual framework of WLB needs to be broadened. Increase in working hours during the last decades of the 20th century contributed significantly towards the development of the WLB construct.
148	(Major, Klein, & Ehrhart, 2002) QT	512 employees from fortune 500 companies, U.S.A.	Work interference with family has relationship with depression, somatic complaint, work overload, and organisational expectations.
149	(Hill, Hawkins, Ferris, & Weitzman, 2001) QT	6451 employees from IBM, U.S.A.	Perceived work flexibility has an association with improved WLB. Perceived work flexibility is beneficial for both the employees as well as for employer. Furthermore, work flexibility is very much useful for employees who are having parental responsibility.

150	(Saltzstein, Ting, & Saltzstein, 2001) QT	32103 Government employees, U.S.A.	Variables such as JS, age, and gender have relationship with WLB. The relationship between family-friendly policies and WLB is influenced by employee demographics.
151	(Tausig & Fenwick, 2001) QT	2953 employees from the U.S.A.	Parental status has a relationship with work-life imbalance. Hours of work can predict work-life imbalance significantly. Whereas, control over work hour enhances the level of WLB. Young and educated perceive increased work-life imbalance.
152	(Allen, Herst, Bruck, & Sttton, 2000) QL	Literature review to identify the consequences of WFC.	Categorised the consequences of work-family conflict into three categories viz., work related outcomes such as job satisfaction, organisational commitment, turnover intention, absenteeism, job performance, career satisfaction and career success; network related outcomes such as life satisfaction, marital satisfaction, family satisfaction and leisure satisfaction; and stress related outcomes such as psychological strain, depression, substance abuse, burnout, work-related stress, family-related stress and somatic/physical symptoms.

153	(Carlson, Kacmar, & Williams, 2000)	1211 respondents from five differential samples, U.S.A.	Developed and validated (content, construct, discriminant and internal reliability) a multidimensional 18 item to measure work-family conflict. The scale has got six dimensions, three (time, strain and behavior) in each direction (i.e., work to family and family to work)
154	(Clark, 2000) QL	Grounded theory	Introduced border theory of WLB. According to border theory, individuals are required to cross the border between various life domains (work and family) simultaneously in order to carry out life activities. Level of domain integration, segmentation, and cross border relationship determines the employee work-life balance level.
155	(Edwards & Rothbard, 2000) QL	Conceptual study	The exchange that takes place in between work and family domain can be of six types viz., compensation, segmentation, spillover, congruence, conflict, and resource drain.
156	(Milkie & Peltola, 1999) QT	469 randomly selected subsample form General Social Survey, 1996, U.S.A.	WFB is a gender-neutral phenomenon. For men work-life imbalance is predicted by hours of work, spouse work hours, unfairness in sharing home responsibility and marital unhappiness. Whereas for women predictors of work-family imbalance were

			marital unhappiness, sacrifice at home and presence of the young kid.
157	(Frone, Yardley, & Markel, 1997) QT	372 employed adults from an organisation (Ontario) who were parents, Canada	There is an inverse relationship between WFC and FWC. Similarly, the relationship between work performance and WFC is also inverse in nature. Distress, overload, and commitment act as mediators in between WFC and FWC. Social support doesn't have any influence either on WFC or on FWC.
158	(Lewis, 1997) QL	Conceptual work aimed at exploring the legal frame work for work-family balance, U.K.	Employees should be provided with flexible work options. The existing labour health and safety laws need to be redefined in order to inculcate work flexibility. Work-life balance policies should be made as an employee right rather than organisational kind.
159	(Lewis & Lewis, 1997) QT	Conceptual work intends to explore the family friendly policies, U.K.	Family-friendly policies were only availed by marginals. Governmental intervention is essential for the proper administration of family-friendly policies in organisations. Family-friendly policies enable the employees to serve the family without sacrificing career advancement.
160	(Netemeyer, Boles, & McMurrian, 1996) QT	Three separate study with a sample of 182 school teachers,	A ten itemised two dimensional (work-to-family conflict as well as family-to-work conflict) scale to

		162 small business owners and 186 sales personals from, Georgia. U.S.A.	measure work-family conflict has been developed.
161	(Thomas & Ganster, 1995) QT	398 health care professionals (having kids < 16 years old) from Nebraska, U.S.A.	Organisational work-family supportive practices have a positive relationship with employee's perception of control over work. Similarly, the supportive practices have a positive relationship with employee's perception about control over work.
162	(Frone, Russell, & Cooper, 1992) QT	An interview of 631 residents of NY, U.S.A.	Found that the employees experience WFC more often than FWC. Whereas, gender has no effect on conflict. The family boundary is more permeable in comparison with work boundary.
163	(Frone, Russell, & Cooper, 1992) Mixed	Surveyed 1933 adults residing in NY, U.S.A., and interviewed 1616 individuals who were surveyed before.	There's a positive relationship between WFC and FWC. Job status (white collar and blue collar job) has a relationship with conflict. Whereas gender and entity have no association with conflict.
164	(Greenhaus & Beutell, 1985) QL	Theoretical study	Identified three types of conflict between work and family viz., time, strain and behavior.
165	(Staines, 1980) QL	Theoretical study	Spillover occurs more often than compensation between work and family domain. Personality type is a potential

<table>
<tr><td></td><td></td><td></td><td>influencer of work and non-work activities. The relationship among work and non-work variables are not consistent across studies.</td></tr>
</table>

References

Abdullah, A. S., Aremu, N. S., & Abogunrin, A. P. (2018). Work-Life Balance and Academic Staff Performance in Nigerian Universities. *Ilorin Journal of Human Resource Management*, 102-113.

Abe, E. N., Fields, Z., & Abe, I. I. (2016). The Efficacy of Wellness Programmes as Work-Life Balance Strategies in the South African Public Service . *Journal of Economics and Behavioral Studies, 8*(6), 52-67.

Ajay K.R, S., & Amanjot, S. (2012). Work Life Balance and Subjective Well Being: A Comparative Study in Public and Private Institutes in Higher Education.

Albertsen, K., Rafnsdóttir, G. L., Grimsmo, A., Tómasson, K., & Kauppinen, K. (2008). Workhours and worklife balance. *SJWEH Suppl*, 14-21.

Allen, T. D., Herst, D. E., Bruck, C. S., & Sttton, M. (2000). Consequences Associated With Work-to-Family Conflict:A Review and Agenda for Future Research. *Journal of Occupational Health Psychology, 5*(2), 278-308. doi:10.1037//1076-8998.5.2.278

Amber, T., Hassan, D. A., Anam, S., & Asif, T. (2012, January). Work-Life Balance as a best practice Model of Human Rerource Management: A Win Win Situational Tool for the Employees and Organisations. *Mediterranean Journal of Social Sciences, 3*(1), 577-584. doi:10.5901/mjss.2012.03.01.577

Antai, D., Oke, A., Braithwaite, P., & Anthony, D. (2015). A 'Balanced' Life: WorkLife Balance and Sickness Absence in Four Nordic Countries. *IJOEM, 6*(4), 205-225. Retrieved from www.theijoem.com

Atheya, R., & Arora, R. (2013). Work-Life Balance (WLB); A Cause of Concern in Banking Sector. *International Journal of Research in Commerce, Economics & Management*, 42-46.

Ayudhya, U. C., Prouska, R., & Beauregard, A. (2017). The Impact of Global Economic Crisis and Austerity on Quality of Working Life and Work-LifeBalance:ACapabilitiesPerspective. *European Management Review*. doi:10.1111/emre.12128

Azeem, S. M., & Akhtar, N. (2014). The Influence of Work Life Balance and Job Satisfaction on Organizational Commitment of Healthcare Employees. *International Journal of Human Resource Studies, 4*(2), 18-24. doi:10.5296/ijhrs.v4i2.5667

Bansal, A. K., & Raj, L. (2017). A Study on Work Life Balance of Women Employees in Indian Oil Corporation Limited Mathura (U.P .). *CPUH-Research Journal*, 6-11. Retrieved from http://www.cpuh.in/academics/academic_journals.php

Banu, A. R. (2015). A Structural Equation Model-I for Work-Life Balance of IT professionals in Chennai. *European Journal of Business and Management, 7*(4), 221-229. Retrieved from www.iiste.org

Banu, A. R., & Duraipandian, K. (2014). Development of an Insrument to measure Work Life Balance of IT Professionals in Chennai. *International Journal of Management, 5*(11), 21-31. Retrieved from http://www.iaeme.com/IJM.asp

Beauregard, T. A., & Henry, L. C. (2007). Making the link between work-life balance practices and organizational performance. *Human resource management review*, 9-22. doi:10.1016/j.hrmr.2008.09.001

Beha, B., Drobnič, S., Präg, P., Baierl, A., & Eckner, J. (2018). Part-time work and gender inequality in Europe: a comparative analysis of satisfaction with work–life balance. *European Societies*. doi:10.1080/14616696.2018.1473627

Bell, A. S., Rajendran, D., & Theiler, S. (2012). Job Stress, Wellbeing, Work-Life Balance and Work-Life Conflict Among Australian Academics. *Electronic Journal of Applied Psychology*, 25-37.

Bharathy, A. (2012). A Perceptual Analysis of Employee Work Life Balance in ITES/BPO Sector. *South Asian Journal of Marketing and Management Research, 2*(7), 12-25. Retrieved from http://www.saarj.com

Brough, P., Siu, O. L., O'Driscoll, M., & Timmis, C. (2015). Work–family enrichment and satisfaction: The mediating role of self-efficacy and work–life balance . *The International Journal of Human Resource Management*. doi:10.1080/09585192.2015.1075574

Brough, P., Timmsb, C., O'Driscollc, M. P., Kalliathd, T., Siue, O.-L., Sitf, C., & Log, D. (2014, March). Work–life balance: a longitudinal evaluation of a new measure across Australia and New Zealand workers. *The International Journal of Human Resource Management, 25*(19), 2724-2744. doi:10.1080/09585192.2014.899262

Bulger, C. A., Matthews, R. A., & Hoffman, M. E. (2007). Work and Personal Life Boundary Management: Boundary Strength, Work/Personal Life Balance, and the Segmentation–Integration Continuum. *Journal of Occupational Health Psychology*, 365-375. doi:10.1037/1076-8998.12.4.365

Carlson, D. S., Grzywacz, J. G., & Zivnuska, S. (2009, October). Is work–family balance more than conflict and enrichment? *National Institute of Health, 62*(10), 1-20. doi:10.1177/0018726709336500

Carlson, D. S., Kacmar, K. M., & Williams, L. J. (2000). Construction and Initial Validation of a Multidimensional Measure of Work–Family Conflict. *Journal of Vocational Behavior, 56*, 249-276. doi:10.1006/jvbe.1999.1713

Carlson, D. S., Kacmar, K. M., Wayne, J. H., & Grzywacz, J. G. (2006). Mesuring the positive side of the work-family interface: Development and validation of a work-family enrichment scale. *Journal of Vocational Behavior , 68*, 131-164. doi:10.1016/j.jvb.2005.02.002

Casper, W. J., Vaziri, H., Wayne, J. H., DeHauw, S., & Greenhaus, J. (2017). The Jingle-Jangle of Work–Nonwork Balance: A Comprehensive and Meta-Analytic Review of Its Meaning and Measurement. *Journal of Applied Psychology*. doi:10.1037/apl0000259

Chandarasekar, K. S., S, S., Nair, R. S., & Ansu.S.R. (2013). Study on Work-Life Balance among the executives in IT Industry with special reference to Technopark, Trivandrum, Kerala. *Asian Journal of Multidimensional Research, 2*(3).

Chandra, V. (2012). Work–life balance: eastern and western perspectives. *The International Journal of Human Resource Management, 23*(5), 1040-1056.

Chitra Devi, A., & Sheela Rani, S. (2012). Work-Life Balance as a Determinant of Life Satisfaction and Family Satisfaction - A Study among Women in BPO. *International Journal on Information Science and Computing, 6*(1), 15-20.

Choa, E., & Allen, T. D. (2018). The transnational family: A typology and implications for workfamily balance. *Human Resource Management Review*. doi:10.1016/j.hrmr.2018.01.001

Cholasseri, S., & Senthilkumar, R. (2017). Work-Life Balance of College Teachers in Malapuram City. *IJARIIE*, 3843-3854.

Clark, S. C. (2000). Work/Family Border Theory: A New Theory of Work/Family Balance. *Human Relations*, 747-770. doi:10.1177/0018726700536001

Coughlan, D. A. (2005). *WORK-LIFE BALANCE An introduction to work-life balance issues and a preliminary exploration of work-life balance culture in NUI, Maynooth.* Equality Authority. Maynooth : Dr. Ann Coughlan.

Dhanya, J., & Kinslin, D. (2017, January 30). *A study on work life balance of women employees at ULCCS Ltd, Kozhkode.* Retrieved from Resrarchgate.net: https://www.researchgate.net/publication

Dhanya.J.S, & Kinslin.D. (2016). A Study on Work Life Balance of Teachers in Engineering Colleges in Kerala. *Journal of Chemical and Pharmaceutical Sciences, 9*(4), 2098-2104.

Dhanya.S, & Ravi, N. (2017). Work Life Balance of Women Faculty in Professional Colleges of Kerala. *Proceedings of International Conference on Strategies in Volatile and Uncertain Environment for Emerging Markets* (pp. 136-144). New Delhi: Indian Institute of Technology Delhi.

Direnzo, M. S., Greenhaus, J. H., & Weer, C. H. (2016, May). Relationship between Protean Career Orientation and Work-Life Balance: A Resource Perspective. *Journal of Organizational Behavior*, 4-57.

Doble, N., & Supriya, M. (2010). Gender Differences in the Perception of Work-Life Balance. *Management*, 331-342.

Edwards, J. R., & Rothbard, N. P. (2000). Mechanisms linking Work and Family: Clarifying the relationhip between Work and Family Constructs. *Academy of Management Review, 25*(1), 178-199.

Emslie, C., & Hunt, K. (2009). 'Live to Work' or 'Work to Live'? A Qualitative Study of Gender and Work–life Balance among Men and Women in Mid-life. *Gender, Work and Organization, 16*(2), 151-172.

Eraranta, K. (2015). A new Social Risk? Social-Scientific Knowledge and Work-Life Balance in Twentieth-Century Finland. *Social Science History*, 63-83. doi:10.1017/ssh.2015.42

Fatima, N., & A.Sahibzada, S. (2012). An Empirical Analysis of Factors Affecting Work Life Balance among University Teachers: The case of Pakistan. *Journal of International Academic Research*, 16-28.

Felstead, A., Jewson, N., Phizacklea, A., & Walters, S. (2002). Opportunities to work at home in the context of work-life balance. *Human Resource Management Journal*, 54-76.

Fisher, G. G., Bulger, C. A., & Smith, C. S. (2009). Beyond Work and Family: A Measure of Work/Nonwork Interference and Enhancement. *Journal of Occupational Health Psychology*, 441-456.

Fisher, K., & Layte, R. (2004). Measuring work-life balance using time diary data. *Electronic International Journal of Time Use Research, 1*(1), 1-13. doi:dx.doi.org/10.13085/eIJTUR.1.1

Fisher-McAuley, G., Stanton, J. M., Jolton, J. A., & Gavin, J. (2003). Modeling the Relationship between Work/Life Balance and Organizational Outcomes. 1-30. Retrieved August 8, 2016, from https://www.researchgate.net/publication/260516221

Fleetwood, S. (2006). *Why work-life balance now?* Lancaster: Lancaster University Management School.

Frone, M. R., Russell, M., & Cooper, M. L. (1992). Antecedents and Outcomes of Work-Family Conflict: Testing a Model of the Work-Family Interface. *Journal of Applied Psychology, 77*(1), 65-78. doi:10.1037//0021-9010.77.1.65

Frone, M. R., Russell, M., & Cooper, M. L. (1992). Prevalence of workfamily conflict: Are work and family boundaries asymmetrically permeable? *Journal of Organizational Behavior*, 723-729.

Frone, M. R., Yardley, J. K., & Markel, K. S. (1997). Developing and Testing an Integrative Model of the Work–Family Interface. *Journal of Vocational Behavior*, 145-167.

Ganiyu, I., Fields, Z., & Atiku, S. (2017). Work-life balance strategies, work-family satisfaction and employees' job performance in Lagos, Nigeria's manufacturing sector. *Journal of Contemporary Management*, 441-460.

Gatrell, C. J., & Cooper, C. L. (2008). Work-life balance: working for whom? *European Journal of International Management, 2*(6), 71-86. Retrieved from www.inderscience.com/ejim

Ghanbaria, A., Ramazanib, M., & Jaliliniac, M. (2013). Analysis of work-life balance from the viewpoint of Iranian accountants. *Management Science Letters* , 2315-2322.

Greenhaus, J. H., & Beutell, N. J. (1985). Sources of Conflict between Work and Family Roles. *The Academy of Management Review, 10*(1), 76-88. Retrieved April 8, 2016, from http://www.jstor.org/stable/258214

Greenhaus, J. H., & Powell, G. N. (2006). When the Work and Family are Allies: A Theory of Work-Family Enrichment. *Academy of Management Review, 31*(1), 72-92.

Greenhaus, J. H., Collins, K. M., & Shaw, J. D. (2003). The relation between work-life balance and quality of life. *Journal of Vocational Behavior*, 510-531. doi:10.1016/S0001-8791(02)00042-8

Greubel, J., Arlinghaus, A., Nachreiner, F., & Lombardi, D. A. (2016). Higher risks when working unusual times? A cross-validation of the effects on safety, health, and work–life balance. *International Archives of Occupational and Environmental Health*. doi:10.1007/s00420-016-1157-z

Grzywacz, J. G., & Bass, B. L. (2003). Work, family, and mental health: Testing different models of work-family fit. *Journal of Marriage and Family*, 248-261.

Grzywacz, J., & Dawn S. Carlson. (2007, November). Conceptualizing Work–Family Balance: Implications for Practice and Research. *Advances in Developing Human Resources, 9*(4), 455-471. doi:10.1177/1523422307305487

Guest, D. E. (2002). Perspectives on the Study of Work-life Balance. *Social Science Information, 42*(2), 255-279. doi:10.1177/0539018402041002005

Haar, J. M., & Bardoel, A. (2007). Work Family Positive Spillover Predicting Outcomes: A study of Australian Employees. Victoria: Australian Centre for Research in Employment and Work.

Haslam, D., Filus, A., Morawska, A., Sanders, M. R., & Fletcher, R. (2014, June). The Work–Family Conflict Scale (WAFCS): Development and Initial Validation of a Self-report Measure of Work–Family Conflict for Use with Parents. *Child Psychiatry and Human Development*. doi:10.1007/s10578-014-0476-0

Hayman, J. (2005). Psychometric Assessment of an Instrument Designed to Measure Work Life Balance. *Research and Practice in Human Resource Management, 13*(1), 85-91.

Hill, E. J., Hawkins, A. J., Ferris, M., & Weitzman, M. (2001). Finding an Extra Day a Week: The Positive Influence of Perceived Job Flexibility on Work and Family Life Balance. *Family Relations*, 49-58.

Hilla, E. J., Grzywaczb, J. G., Allena, S., Blancharda, V. L., Matz-Costac, C., Shulkinc, S., & Pitt-Catsouphesc, M. (2008). Defining and conceptualizing workplace flexibility. *Community, Work & Family*, 149-163. doi:10.1080/13668800802024678

Hirschi, A., Shockley, K. M., & Zacher, H. (in press). Achieving work-family balance: An action regulation model. *Academy of Management Review*.

Jayakar, T. J., & Babu, S. S. (2012). Professional Communication for Better Work-Life Balance. *Journal of Education and Practice, 3*(6), 37-46. Retrieved from www.iiste.org

Jindal, M. (2016). A Study on Work-life Balance of Working Women in Service Sector. *International Journal of Research in Finance and Marketing*, 14-21.

Kacmar, K. M., Crawford, W. S., Carlson, D. S., Ferguson, M., & Whitten, D. (2014). A Short and Valid Measure of Work-Family Enrichment. *Journal of Occupational Health Psychology, 19*(1), 32-45. doi:10.1037/a0035123

Kalliath, P., Kalliath, T., Chan, X. W., & Chan, C. (2018). Linking Work–Family Enrichment to Job Satisfaction through Job Well-Being and Family Support: A Moderated Mediation 5Analysis of Social Workers across India. *British Journal of Social Work*, 1-22.

Kalliath, T., & Brough, P. (2008). Work–life balance: A review of the meaning of the balance construct. *Journal of Management & Organization , 14*(3), 323-327.

Kar, S., & Misra, K. C. (2013). Nexus between Work Life Balance Practices and Employee Retention – The Mediating Effect of a Supportive Culture. *Asian Social Science, 9*(11), 63-69. doi:10.5539/ass.v9n11p63

Kaur, J. (2013). WORK-LIFE BALANCE: ITS CORRELATION WITH SATISFACTION WITH LIFE AND PERSONALITY DIMENSIONS AMONGST COLLEGE TEACHERS. *International Journal of Marketing, Financial Services & Management Research, 8*(2), 24-35. Retrieved from www.indianresearchjournals.com

Keeton, K., Fenner, D. E., Johnson, T. R., & Hayward, R. A. (2007). Predictors of Physician Career Satisfaction, Work–Life Balance, and Burnout. *Obetetrics & Gynecology*, 949-955.

Kumari, S., & Selvi, A. (2015). An Exploratory Study Of Work Life Balance Emanates And Work Satisfaction In Ericsson Company-Chennai City. *International Journal of scientific research and management (IJSRM)*, 3565-3571.

Kurowska, A. (2018). Gendered Effects of Home-Based Work on Parents' Capability to Balance Work with Non-work: Two Countries with Different Models of Division of Labour Compared. *Social Indicators Research*. doi:10.1007/s11205-018-2034-9

Lakshmi, K. S., Ramachandran, T., & Boohene, D. (2012). Analysis of Work Life Balance of Female Nurses in Hospitals - Comparative Study between Government and Private Hospital in Chennai, TN., India. *International Journal of Trade, Economics and Finance*, 213-218.

Lakshmipriya, & Krishna, R. (2016). Work Life Balance and Implications Of Spill Over Theory – A Study on Women Entrepreneurs. *International Journal of Research in IT & Management*, 96-109.

Lavassani, K. M., & Movahedi, B. (2014). Developments in Theories And Measures of Work-Family Relationships: From Conflict to Balance. *Contemporary Research on Organization Management and Administration, 2*(1), 6-18.

Lazar, I., Osoian, C., & Ratiu, P. (2010). The Role of Work-Life Balance Practices in Order to Improve Organizational Performance. *European Research Studies*, 201-214.

Leaptrott, J., & McDonald, J. M. (2011). The conflict between work and family roles: the effects on managers' reliance on information sources in dealing with significant workplace events. *Journal of Organizational Culture, Communications and Conflict*, 132-148.

Lewis, S. (1997). 'Family Friendly' Employment Policies: A Route to Changing Organizational Culture or Playing About at the Margins? *Gender Work and Organization*, 13-23. doi:10.1111/1468-0432.00020

Lewis, S., & Lewis, J. (1997). Work, family and well-being. Can the law help? (P. Taylor, Ed.) *Legal and Criminological Psychology, 2*(2), 155-167. doi:10.1111/j.2044-8333.1997.tb00340.x

Lewis, S., Gambles, R., & Rapoport, R. (2007). The constraints of a 'work–life balance' approach: an international perspective. *International Journal of Human Resource*, 360-373.

Li, Y. (2018). Effects of Work-Life Balance on Organizational Commitment: A Study in China's State-Owned Enterprise. *World Journal of Social Science Research*, 144-166. doi:10.22158/wjssr.v5n2p144

Lockwood, N. R. (2003). Work/Life Balance: Challenges and Solutions. *SHRM Research Quarterly*.

Lyness, K. S., & Judiesch, M. K. (2014). Gender Egalitarianism and Work–Life Balance for Managers: Multisource Perspectives in 36 Countries. *Appilied Psychology: An International Review*, 96-129. doi:10.1111/apps.12011

Major, V. S., Klein, K. J., & Ehrhart, M. G. (2002). Work Time, Work Interference With Family, and Psychological Distress. *Journal of Applied Psychology, 87*(3), 427-436. doi:10.1037//0021-9010.87.3.427

Malik, M. I., Zaheer, A., Khan, M. A., & Ahmed, M. (2010). Developing and Testing a Model of Burnout at Work and Turnover Intensions among Doctors in Pakistan. *International Journal of Business and Management, 5*(10), 234-247. Retrieved from www.ccsenet.org/ijbm

Mathew, R. V., & Panchanatham, N. (2011). An Exploratory study on the Work-Life Balance of Women Entrepreneures in South India. *Asian Academy of Management Journal*, 77-105.

Mazerolle, S. M., & Goodman, A. (2013). Fulfillment of Work–Life Balance From the Organizational Perspective: A Case Study. *Journal of Athletic Training, 48*, 668-667. doi:10.4085/1062-6050-48.3.24

McMillan, H. S., Morris, M. L., & Atchley, E. K. (2008). Constructs of the Work/Life Interface and their Importance to HRD. *Academy of Human Resource Development International Research Conference in the Americas.* Panama: ERIC.

McNamaraa, T. K., Pitt-Catsouphesa, M., Matz-Costaa, C., Brownb, M., & Valcourc, M. (2013). Across the continuum of satisfaction with work–family balance: Work hours, flexibility-fit, and work–family culture. *Social Science Research*, 283-298.

Meenakshi, A., & Bhuvaneshwari, M. (2013). Work Organisation and Work-Life Balance in the BPO Sector. *International Journal of Scientific and Research Publications, 3*(6), 1-4.

Meenakshi, S. P., Subrahmanyam, C. V., & Ravichandran, K. (2013). The Importance of Work-Life-Balance. *IOSR Journal of Business and Management*, 31-35.

Milkie, M. A., & Peltola, P. (1999). Playing All the Roles: Gender and the Work-Family Balancing Act. *Journal of Marriage and the Family, 61*(2), 476-490. Retrieved from http://www.jstor.org/stable/353763

Monica.M. (2015, June). A study on work life balance at State Bank of Mysore. *International Journal of in Multidisciplinary and Academic Research (SSIJMAR), 4*(3), 1-15. Retrieved from www.ssijmar.in

Morganson, V. J., Litano, M. L., & O'Neill, S. K. (2014). Promoting Work–Family Balance Through Positive Psychology: A Practical Review of the Literature. *The Psychologist-Manager Journal, 17*(4), 221-244. doi:10.1037/mgr0000023

Mugeanyi, N. (2017, July). *Work Life Balance: The Need for Self Awareness and Care*. Retrieved from Researchgate.net: https://www.researchgate.net/publication/318910632

Muthukumar, M., Savitha, R., & Kannadas, P. (2014). Work LIFE Balance. *Global Journal of Finance and Management, 6*(9), 827-832.

Naithani, P. (2010). Overview of Work-Life Balance Discourse and Its Relevance in Current Economic Scenario. *Asian Social Science*, 148-155. Retrieved from www.ccsenet.org/ass

Netemeyer, R. G., Boles, J. S., & McMurrian, R. (1996). Development and Validation of Work-Family Conflict and Family-Work Conflict Scales. *Journal of Applied Psychology, 81*(4), 400-410.

Orkibi, H., & Brandta, Y. I. (2015). HowPositivityLinksWithJobSatisfaction:PreliminaryFindingsonthe MediatingRoleofWork-LifeBalance. *Europe's Journal of Psychology, 11*(3), 406-418. doi:10.5964/ejop.v11i3.869

Otis, E. (2009). TheParadoxofFlexibility:Guilt,Regret,andWork/Life BalanceforToday'sMother. *Advances in Communication Theory & Research*, 2-35.

Otusile, E., Ibeh, J. M., & Ndubuisi, U. (2017). Finding Sustainable Balance Between Your Work And Personal Life. *International Journal of Innovative Research and Advanced Studies*, 328-332.

Owens, J., Kottwitz, C., Tiedt, J., & Ramirez, J. (2018). Strategies to Attain Faculty Work-Life BalancE. *Building Healthy Academic Communities Journal*, 58-73.

Padmanabhan, M., & Kumar, S. S. (2016). Work-Life Balance and Work-Life Conflict on Career Advancement of Women Professionals in Information and Communication Technology Sector, Bengaluru, India. *International Journal of Research*, 119-130. doi:10.5281/zenodo.56642

Pandu, A., Balu, A., & Poorani, K. (2013). Assessing Work-Life Balance among IT & ITeS Women Professional. *The Indian Journal of Industrial Relations*, 611-620.

Parida, S. K. (2012, June). Measuring the Work Life Balance: An Inter-Personal study of the employees in IT and ITes Scctor. *An International Business Research Journal, 1*(1), 79-90. Retrieved from www.jbmcr.org

Parker, C. C., & Citera, M. (2010). Changing Roles: Are Millennials Redefining Work-Life Balance. Atlanta: Society for Industrial-Organizational Psychology.

Patwa, P. (2011). Work Life Balance: A cross sectional study of Banking & Insurance Sector. *International Journal of Research in Commerce, IT & Management*, 85-91.

Poelmans, S. A., Kalliath, T., & Brough, P. (2008). Achieving work–life balance: Current theoretical and practice issues. *Journal of Management & Organization*, 227-238. doi:10.1017/S1833367200003242

Poulose, S., & Sudarsan.N. (2014). Work Life Balance: A Conceptual Review. *International Journal of Advances in Management and Economics, 3*(2), 1-17. Retrieved from www.managementjournal.info

Powell, G. N., & Greenhaus, J. H. (2006). THINK PIECE Is the opposite of positive negative? Untangling the complex relationship between work-family enrichment and conflict. *Career Development International, 11*(7), 650-659. doi:10.1108/13620430610713508

Pradhan, R. K., Jena, L. K., & Kumari, I. G. (2016). Effect of Work-Life Balance on Organizational Citizenship Behaviour: Role of Organisational Commitment. *Global Business Review*, 1-15. doi:10.1177/0972150916631071

Prithi, S., & Vasumathi, A. (2018). The Influence of Demographic Profile on Work Life Balance of Women Employees in Tannery Industry – An Empirical Study. *Pertanika J. Soc. Sci. & Hum*, 259-284.

Raj, A. E., & Julius, S. (2015). Working Father and their Perceived Work – Life Balance with Special Reference to Hyundai Motors (I) Private Limited at Chennai. *International Journal of Advanced Scientific Research & Development*, 54-63.

Raj.R, A. (2013). A Study on Work-Life Balance of Employees in Pharma Marketing. *International Research Journal of Pharmacy*, 209-211.

Raj.R, A., & Ramanathan, H. N. (2012). A Study of Work-Life Balance of Paramedical Employees with Special Reference to a Private Hospital. *Indian Journal of Commerce & Management Studies*, 74-79.

Raju, G. (2012). Work-Life Balancing Activities: Implications and Solutions. *International Journal of Social Science and Interdisciplinary Research*, 34-44.

Rania, S., Kamalanabhan, & Selvarania. (2011). Work-Life Balance Reflections on Employee Satisfaction. *Serbian Journal of Management*, 85-96.

Rao, M. V. (2015). The influence of Personal and Demographic Factors on Work-Life Balance of Employees in Corporate Sector. *Pezzottaite Journals*, 1815-1822.

Ratna, R., Gupta, N., Devani, K., & Chawla, S. (2011, November). Work-Life Balance in BPO Sector. *International Journal of Physical and Social Science, 1*(3), 79-107. Retrieved from http://www.ijmra.us

Ravikumar, T. (2011). A Study on Work-Life Balance of BPO Employees in India. *International Journal of Research in IT, Management and Engineering*, 174-193.

Reddy, N. K., Vranda, M. N., Ahmed, A., Nirmala, B. P., & Siddaramu, B. (2010). Work–Life Balance among Married Women Employees. *Indian Journal of Psychological Medicine*, 112-118. doi:10.4103/0253-7176.78508

Rennar, H. (2007). In search of true work/life balance: in order to consistently attain work/life balance, we must change our work ethic and corporate culture through education, acceptance, communication and accountability.(YOUR CAREER). *Financial Executive*. Retrieved from https://www.highbeam.com/doc/1G1-162875480.html

Renthlei, L., & Singh, A. K. (2015). Impact of Demographic Variables on Work-Life Balance of Teachers: A Study of Private Unaided Schools in Aizawl West Region of Mizoram in India. *Pezzottaite Journals*, 1920-1926.

Rincy, V., & Panchanatham, N. (2010). Development of A Psychometric Instrument to Measure Work-life Balance. *Continental J. Social Sciences*, 50-58.

Sakthivel, D., & Jayakrishnan, J. (2010). Work life balance and Organizational commitment for Nurses. *Asian Journal of Business and Management Sciences, 2*(5), 1-6.

Saltzstein, A. L., Ting, Y., & Saltzstein, G. H. (2001). Work-Family Balance and Job Satisfaction: The Impact of Family-Friendly Policies on Attitudes of Federal Government Employees. *Public Administration Review*, 452-467. doi:10.1111/0033-3352.00049

Shanafelt, T. D., Boone, S., Tan, L., Dyrbye, L. N., Sotile, W., Satele, D., . . . Oreskovich, M. R. (2012). Burnout and Satisfaction With Work-Life Balance Among US Physicians Relative to the General US Population. *Arch Inters Med*, 501-509.

Sharma, B., & Nair, M. (2015). Work-Life Balance among Working Women in Service Sectors: A Conceptual Framework. *Pezzottaite Journals*, 1912-1917.

Sharma, J. K., & Mehta, D. (2009). A Study on Impact of Work-Life Balance Issues on Performance of Pharma Sales Managers.

Sheokand, K. S., & Priyanka. (2013). Work Life Balance: An Overview of Indian Companies. *International Journal of Research in Commerce and Management*, 138-143.

Shiva, G. (2013). A Study on Work Family Balance and Challenges Faced By Working Women. *IOSR Journal of Business and Management, 14*(5), 1-4. Retrieved from www.iosrjournals.org

Simonea, S. D., Agusa, M., Lasioa, D., & Serria, F. (2018). Development and Validation of a Measure of Work-Family Interface. *Journal of Work and Organizational Psychology*. doi:10.5093/jwop2018a19

Singh, S. (2013). Work - Life Balance: A Literature Review. *Global Journal of Commerce & Management Perspective, 2*(3), 84-91.

Singh, S. (2014). Mesuring Work-life Balance in India. *International Journal of Advance Research in Computer Science and Management Studies, 2*(5), 35-43. Retrieved from www.ijarcms.com

Sinha, D. (2014). Study of Work Life Balance @ CCIL (India), NOIDA. *Journal of Management Sciences And Technology*, 8-14.

Smeltzer, S. C., Cantrell, M. A., Sharts-Hopko, N. C., Heverly, M. A., Jenkinson, A., & Nthenge, S. (2016, April). Psychometric Analysis of the Work/Life Balance Self-Assessment Scale. *Journal of Nursing Measurement, 24*(1), 5-14. doi:10.1891/1061-3749.24.1.5

Smith, J., & Gardner, D. (2007). Factors Affecting Employee Use of Work-Life Balance Initiatives. *New Zealand Journal of Psychology, 32*(1), 3-12.

Solomon, D. J. (2007). The Role of Peer Review for Scholarly Journals in the Information Age. *The Journal of Electronic Publishing, 10*(1). doi:10.3998/3336451.0010.107

Staines, G. L. (1980). Spillover Versus Compensation: A Review of the Literature on the Relationship Between Work and Nonwork. *Human Relations, 33*(2), 111-129. doi:10.1177/001872678003300203

Sturges, J., & Guest, D. (2004). Working to live or living to work? Work/life balance early in the career. *Human Resource Management Journal, 14*(4), 5-20.

Sudha.D, Anitha.S, & Harikumar, P. (2016). Impact of Job Related issues on the Work-Life Balance of Women. *International Journal of Advanced Research in ISSN: 2278-6236 Management and Social Sciences*, 311-329.

Sundaresan, S. (2014). Work-Life Balance-Implication for Working Women. *International Journal of Sustainable Development*, 93-102. Retrieved from http://www.ssrn.com/link/OIDA-Intl-Journal-Sustainable-Dev.html

Suresh, S., & Kodikal, R. (2017). SEM approach to explore Work Life Balance: A study among nurses of Multispecialty Hospitals. *Sahyadri Journal of Management*, 1-16.

Swarnalatha, C., & Rajalakshmi, S. (2015). Examining the Role Of Organization In Providing Healthy Work Life Balance And Its Impact On Psychological Outcomes. In *International Conference on Inter Disciplinary Research in*

Engineering and Technology (pp. 214-221). Retrieved from www.icidret.in

Szener, J. B., Grzankowski, K. S., Eng, K. H., Odunsi, K., & Frederick, P. J. (2016). Evaluation of satisfaction with work-life balance among U.S Gynecologic Oncology Fellows: A cross-sectional study. *Gynecologic Oncology Reports*, 17-20. Retrieved from http://dx.doi.org/10.1016/j.gore.2016.03.001

Talukder, A. H. (2011). A Shifting Paradigm of Work-Life Balance in Service Context-An Empirical Study . *Indus Journal of Management & Social Sciences*, 10-23.

Tambe, S. (2017). Work-life Balance and Gender Bias : A Contrarian View. *International Journal of Business and Management*, 14-16.

Tausig, M., & Fenwick, R. (2001). Unbinding Time: Alternate Work Schedules and Work-Life Balance. *Journal of Family and Economic Issues, 22*(2), 101-119.

Thakur, S., & Surampudi, S. (2011). Attaining Work – Life Balance : Strategies For Increasing Work Productivity. *VSRD International Journal of Business & Management Research, 1*(2), 115-120. Retrieved from www.visualsoftindia.com/journal.html

Thomas, L. T., & Ganster, D. C. (1995). Impact of Family-Supportive Work Variables on Work-Family Conflict and Strain: A Control Perspective. *Journal of Applied Psychology, 80*(1), 6-15.

Thyer, B. A. (2008). The Importance of Journal Articles. In B. A. Thyer, *Preparing Research Articles* (pp. 20-43). New York: Oxford University Press. doi:DOI:10.1093/acprof:oso/9780195323375.003.0001

Timmis, C., Brough, P., Siu, O. L., O'Driscoll, M., & Kalliath, T. (2015). Handbook of research on work-life balance in Asia. In *Cross-cultural impact of work-life balance on health and work outcomes* (pp. 294-314).

Toffoletti, K., & Starr, K. (2016). Women Academics and Work–Life Balance: Gendered Discourses of Work and Care. *Gender, Work & Organization*, 6-20. doi:doi:10.1111/gwao.12133

Umene-Nakano, W., Kato, T. A., Kikuchi, S., Tateno, M., Fujisawa, D., Hoshuyama, T., & Nakamura, J. (2013). Nationwide Survey of Work Environment, Work-Life Balance and Burnout among Psychiatrists in Japan. *Plos One, 8*(2), 1-8.

Valcour, M. (2007). Work-Based Resources as Moderators of the Relationship Between Work Hours and Satisfaction With Work-Family Balance. *Journal of Applied Psychology, 92*(6), 1512-1523. doi:10.1037/0021-9010.92.6.1512

Vanishree. (2012, November). Work-life Balance in the BPO Sector. *Journal of Business Management and Social Science Research, 1*(2), 35-39. Retrieved from www.borjournals.com

Vijayalakshmi, B., & Latha, G. (2013). Work Life Balance: A Study on University Faculty of Sri Padmavathi Mahila Visvavidyalam, Tirupathi. *International Journal of Commerce, Economics and Management, 3*(4), 37-41. Retrieved from http://ijrcm.org.in/

Villiers, J. D., & Kotze, E. (2003). Work-Life Balance A study in Petroleum Industry. *Journal of Human Resource Management*, 15-23.

Viswanathan, K., & Jeyakumaran. (2013, Auguest). Instrument Development for Studying Work Life Balance Programs in Information Technology Firms. *Journal of Business and Management, 11*(4), 47-53. Retrieved from www.iosrjournals.org

Voydanoff, P. (2005). Toward a Conceptualization of Perceived Work-Family Fit and Balance: A Demands and Resources Approach. *Journal of Marriage and Family*, 822-836.

Waumsley, J. A., Houston, D. M., & Marks, G. (2010). What about Us? Measuring the Work-Life Balance of People Who Do Not Have Children. *Review of European Studies*, 3-17.

White, M., Hill, S., McGovern, P., Mills, C., & Smeaton, D. (2003). 'High-performance' Management Practices, Working Hours and Work–Life Balance. *British Journal of Industrial Relations*, 175-195.

Yadav, R. K., & Dabhade, N. (2013). Work life balance amongst the working women in public sector banks – a case study of State Bank of India. *International Letters of Social and Humanistic Sciences*, 1-22.

Zakaria, A., & Omar, M. K. (2016). Manifestation of work-life balance in the Malaysian banking workforce: Transformational leadership the potent enabler. *7thAsia-Pacific International Conference on Environment-Behaviour Studies*, 279-287. Retrieved from www.e-iph.co.uk

Zakaria, M. F., Mat, N., & Abdullah, A. R. (2018). Pengaruh Personaliti Big Five Kepada Keseimbangan Kerja-Kehidupan: Perspektif Guru. *International Journal of Education, Psychology and Counseling*, 21-31.

CHAPTER - 5

REVIEW - OTHER MATERIALS

"Philosophically, the universe has really never made things in ones. The Earth is special and everything else is different? No, we've got seven other planets. The sun? No, the sun is one of those dots in the night sky. The Milky Way? No, it's one of a hundred billion galaxies. And the universe - maybe it's countless other universes"

-   Neil deGrasse Tyson (Astrophysicist)

Both reviewing the books and reading the review is very imperative, as it helps to get up-to-date with recent progress in the relevant. The task of reviewing book is as important as undertaking the research work (Fleenor, 2004). It's a fact that books were not published often while comparing it with frequency and number of scholarly journals. Though they are limited in number, books incorporate very detailed information about the topic. Through the review of a single book itself, it's possible to get familiarise with a novel topic and have a thoughtful understanding about the same. This particular feature of the books put it ahead and make them eye-catching among academicians. Table 5.1, illustrates the chronological arrangement of various books and other materials reviewed as the part of the study in descending order.

Table 5.1		
Table Showing Review in Terse-Other materials		
No.	Author details	Core theme/idea Proposed
1	(Lewis & Beauregard, 2018)	Defined work-life balance either as an individual experience or aspiration, with particular focus on time-squeezed white collar workers, or as an adjective to describe workplace policies or practices (e.g., flexible work arrangements) or public policies (e.g., parental leave) that purport to enhance these individual experiences (i.e., WLB policies, practices, or supports).
2	(Crawford, 2016), N.Y, U.S.A.	Effective allocation of time and resource is the key to work-life balance. Because of the individualistic nature of the work-life balance concept, it's impossible to frame a common work-life balance policy. Therefore, the work-life balance policy is to be employee-specific and tailor-made.
3	(Trindade, 2016) London, U.K.	Stress is a significant predictor of work-life imbalance. But the element of stress is present in every human activity. Furthermore, the ability to handle stress depends on the cognitive skill and experience of the employee. The author introduced a reason-based approach to curtail stress and thereby reduce the work-life imbalance.
4	(Gora, 2015) Mumbai, India	Methodologies to followed by the employees in order to achieve a satisfactory WLB was the central theme of the book. Understanding about the self and having control over own emotion is the key to WLB.
5	(Tamsett, 2015) U.K.	Described stress as the source of work-life imbalance and therefore, stress management is the best possible solution against work-life imbalance. Furthermore, in order to overcome work-life imbalance one should plan the daily life and review the plan on a daily basis. The book also explains the significance of hobbies

6	(Schwingshackl, 2014) U.S.A.	and recreation time and its potentiality alleviate work-life imbalance. Work-life balance is a superstition imposed by the 21st century corporations with an objective to explore the human resource through the introduction of the family-friendly work environment. The editorial describes how the family-friendly work environment become advantageous for the employer and its allied consequences and misconceptions in favour of corporate citizenship.
7	(Chandaria, 2013) Mumbai, India	Studies the WLB among duel carried couples in the medical sector and found that the duel carried couples in the medical sector have a good level of WLB based on the mean score obtained on WLB scale (Hymans 2005 scale of WLB). The study also found that gender has no effect on WLB.
8	(Carlson, Kacmar, Grzywacz, Tepper, & Whitten, 2013) U.S.A.	With the help of data obtained from 75 supervisors and 205 subordinate staff belongs to the southern U.S.A. analysed the relationship between WFB, organisational citizenship behaviour and positive effect and found that the positive effect acts as an intervening variable that mediates the relationship between WFB and organisational citizenship behaviour.
9	(Furnham, 2013) N.Y, U.S.A.	Identified self-reliance is the basis of WLB. Furthermore, according to the author the WLB has an association with self-confidence, self-control self-esteem and self-efficiency. The book also describes that religiosity and spirituality can be used as a stress management tool.
10	(Greenhaus & Brummelhuis, Models and frameworks underlying work–life research, 2013)	Briefed various work-life balance models in operation and allied methodologies followed by the researchers for the measurement of work-life balance. The authors also filled in the development of work-life balance research from the role theory.

11	(Alboher, 2012) N.Y, U.S.A.	The book describes WLB as a subject which is individualistic in nature. Hence, the responsibility to balance the life between various domain is primarily the responsibility of the employees themselves. Assertiveness is an important cognitive skill that acts as a catalyst in achieving WLB. An individual should consistently put his effort towards his passion at the same time he will also be able to find compactable colleagues, able to follow entertainment and leisure in order to have a WLB.
12	(Banker, 2012) Noida, India	Relationship strength and mutual belongingness with the nearest and dearest were identified as the factors that are responsible for work-life balance.
13	(Eurofound 2012, 2012) Dublin, Ireland.	The majority (83%) of the respondents were satisfied with the current apportionment time between work and non-work activities. Compared to salaried, self-employed have lower satisfaction with regard to the current apportionment time between work and non-work activities. Gender doesn't fount to have any association with WLB perception. Where the life phase of the employee found to have a significant association with WLB perception.
14	(Hutcheson, 2012) Georgia, U.S.A.	Work-life balance is a concept which is dynamic in nature. Because of the dynamic nature of the concept employees should constantly adjust their activities for achieving WLB. Time management is only an antecedent to WLB. According to the author, WLB is the right magnitude of involvement in various activities of the life in such a way one can feel satisfaction and involvement both in the work as well as in the non-work activity.
15	(Employment Market Analysis and Research,	Using data obtained from 2000 employed adults from U.K. analysed the effectiveness of WLB policies and found that the existing WLB policies

	2011) Victoria Street, U.K.	are very effective in managing the WLB of the employees.
16	(Gregory & Milner, 2011) Manchester, U.K.	Lack of organisational level initiatives and programmes to manage work-life balance is a problem need to be addressed. Absence conscience and multiplicity of definitions on work-life balance is another severe issue faced by work-life balance research. The gendered colouring of the subject is another element that limits the scope of work-life balance research. The absence of a national framework to manage WLB is another matter that needs attention.
17	(International Labour Organisation, 2011) Geneva, Switzerland	The important cause of increased work-family friction among women was unequal sharing of caregiving responsibility. Compared to developed economies (E.U. nations), nations belong to Asia, Africa and the Middle East have a wider gap between men and women in terms of time spend for paid and unpaid work (household work). An aging population, health pandemics, inadequate family supportive social policies and shift in work pattern were the hurdles faced by employees in achieving work-life balance.
18	(Kelly, 2011) New York, U.S.A.	Work-life imbalance occurs when the employees are unable to meet the demands of various life domains. There's a need to communicate work-life balance policies to the employees. That is how and when to make use of work-life balance policies. Work-life balance is primarily the responsibility of employees themselves and the organisations provide and assistive framework.
19	(Nomaguchi & Milkie, 2011) Bowling Green, U.S.A.	Based on data obtained from 545 dual dual-earner couples evaluated how the perceived status about the spouse's WFC and its implications on relationship quality and found that the husband overestimates the WLC of his wife, which is, in turn, facilitate relationship quality. Whereas the wife underestimates the

		WLC of her partner, which result in poor relationship quality.
20	(Rantanen, Kinnunen, Mauno, & Tillemann, 2011) Berlin, Germany	Explained the theoretical interlink between work-life balance and the role theory. Furthermore, the authors also describe the relationship between personal psychology and work-life balance. According to the authors, work-life balance is a concept which starts its evolution from the role theory, and concepts such as spillover, conflict, facilitation, enrichment and enhancement were the pathways between role theory and work-life balance.
21	(Ratna, Gupta, Devani, & Chawla, 2011) London, U.K.	Work-life balance can be off for types viz., beneficial balance, harmful balance, active balance, and passive balance. Beneficial balance the presence of work to non-work enhancement together with the absence of work-to non-work conflict. The harmful balance-the absence of work to non-work enhancement together with presence of work-to non-work conflict. Active balance-presence of work to non-work enhancement together with the presence of work to non-work conflict. Passive balance-absence of both work to non-work enhancement as well as conflict.
22	(Reindl, Kaiser, & Stolz, 2011) London, U.K.	Explained the relationship between individual values and resources and its capability to influence the work-life balance experiences. Work-life balance is designated as a concept which is strongly associated with an individual's perception about the ideal work-life conditions. The socio-cultural interlink of work-life balance is also explored in detail.
23	(Shein & Chen, 2011) Rotterdam, Netherlands	Critically evaluated the WLB literature over the past four decades and accounted for the evolution of WLB research from the concept of work-life conflict until the concept of balance.
24	(Blates, Clark, & Chakrabarti,	The theoretical foundation of the WLB concept was the subject matter of discussion. They further

	2010) N.Y, U.S.A.	explained how the boundary theory and border theory interlink with the concept of WLB.
25	(Dewe, O'Driscoll, & Cooper, 2010) Malden, U.S.A.	According to the authors view work-life conflict is the outcome of inter-role stress. They further put forward the proposition that work-life balance is a concept which is more comprehensive than work-family balance. The absence of researchers conscious over WLB definition was also the matter of discussion.
26	(Taylor, 2010) Swindon, U.K.	There's a wide spared need among employees for WLB policy. Smaller firms find it hard to cope up with work-life balance requirements of the employees. Employees will also suppress their need for work-life balance as the because of the economic and social significance of the paid work.
27	(Chang, McDonald, & Burton, 2009) Queensland, Australia	Based on the review of 245 empirical papers on WLB form the period 1978 to 2006 WLB is of recent origin. However, studies pertaining to work-family interactions were very popular during the periods of the 20th century itself. The researchers started to explore work-life balance particularly during the period of 2005. It was only in the researchers have identified there is a need to distinguish the concept of work-family balance from work-life balance.
28	(England, 2009) California, U.S.A.	The author illustrated the benefits available to an organisation through the diversification of its workforce in terms of entity, culture, and gender and its resultant impact of employee work-life balance. The diversification of the workforce, in turn, leads to the diversification of the employee's demands, but the strength of demand will be less and therefore it can be easily managed by the organisation in a satisfactory manner.
29	(Greenberg & Avigdor, 2009)	The successfulness of the work-life balance depends on the ability of the employee to call for help and support when they actually need them.

	New Jersey, U.S.A.	Identification work-life balance need and the ability of the employee to link the identified need against the best possible work-life balance policy in operation is the crucial step in the work-life balance management process.
30	(Haddon, Hede, & Whiteoak, 2009) Australia	Proposed a new model of work-life balance under which work-life balance is proposed as an intervening element that acts as an intervening element between work-family factors and work-family conflict and enrichment. Work-family conflict and enrichment were the immediate consequence of work-life balance/imbalance.
31	(Krings, Nierling, Pedaci, & Piersanti, 2009) Luxembourg, Switzerland	Found that lack of flexibility and long hours of work were the main cause of the work-life imbalance. Furthermore, during the final lap of 20th century organisations become more technical and the jobs become casual. The hand just-in-time approach of production adds flexibility to the organisation but it dismantles the employee security and tenure. Similarly, organisations adopt a 'strategic approach' in human resource management and as a result outsourcing, casualization, downsizing, on-job-call, and stand-by-work become common. Project-oriented work further fuels the work intensification and enhance employee responsibility.
32	(Littig, 2008) Vienna, Austria	Three core themes responsible for the emergence of the work-life balance concept were the feminisation of the work environment, demographic changes and the corporate interest in favour of flexibility.
33	(Maxwell, 2008) Alexandria, U.S.A.	Based on the case study on a series of large organisations the researcher has identified certain themes that promote work-life balance. The themes were: - 1. The management philosophy should be vibrant for employees.

		2. Work should be made fun and good leadership, as well as mentorship, is essential for work-life balance. 3. Transparent job sharing can enhance WLB. 4. Organisational culture and co-worker support influence the WLB. 5. Career break can enhance WLB.
34	(Poelmans, Odle-Dusseau, & Beham, 2008) U.S.A.	Described the etymology of work-life balance and distinguished the concept of balance from enrichment, facilitation, enhancement, spillover, and conflict.
35	(Bloom, Kretschmer, & Reenen, 2006) London, U.K.	With the help of data obtained from 700 firms in the Europe and US, tested the validity of Chirac theory (i.e., positive association between management quality and WLB) and win-win theory (WLB improve productivity). The empirical data doesn't validate either of the theory and WLB is social desirability and has associated cost from the organisational perspective.
36	(Department of Labour New Zealand, 2006) Wellington, New Zealand	Based on the survey of 1100 employers and 2000 employees, found that 56 percent of the New Zealand employees have the work-life imbalance. Extended hours of work, rotating shift and care responsibility has a positive relationship with work-life conflict.
37	(Redmond, Valiulis, & Drew, 2006) Dublin, Ireland	Based on an extensive literature review on WLB with reference to pregnancy and child care, found that work-life balance policies pertaining to work schedule flexibility have an association with WLB. The absence of a regulatory framework to monitor and guide work-life balance policy at national and international level threatens the employee work-life balance.
38	(Thompson, 2006) Toronto, Canada	Employee demographics itself doesn't have the potential to influence the work-life balance, but when it is coupled with contextual factors the demographics it predicts work-life balance.

39	(Visser & Williams, 2006) London, U.K.	With the help of a telephonic interview of 1000 UNISON members, it has been found that compared to job satisfaction work-life balance is less important. The perceived control over work has a relationship with work-life balance.
40	(State Services Commission New Zealand , 2005) Wellington, New Zealand	Work-life balance is the joint responsibility of employees, organisations, and government. Defined work-life balance as the interaction between paid work with non-work in such a way that the tension between work and non-work activities were at a minimum. Self-assessment and self-appraisal is the key to WLB.
41	(Smithson & Stokoe, 2005) Malden, U.S.A.	Found that work-life balance is a concept which is nicked by the feminist paradigm. Work-life balance is earmarked as a topic pertaining to the work and family integration of women employees. The work-life balance need of men was ignored not only by the organisations and the society but also by the researchers too.
42	(Vlems, 2005) Geel, Belgium	The author claims that the issue of work-life imbalance emerges as a consequence of the changes that occurred in the socio-cultural environment during the 20th century such as aging population, sandwich generation, atypical job culture and feminization of workforce.
43	(Yuile, Chang, & Gudmundsson, 2005) Brisbane, Australia	Based on data obtained from 1241 employed people from Australian, found that there's an association between perceived work flexibility and work-life balance. The employee who perceived to have work-flexibility have work-life balance and vice versa. Whereas, alternative work arrangements, career facilities, and offsite work arrangements failed to found any association with work-life balance.
44	(Oxford Brookes University, 2004) U.K	Based on data obtained from 492 employees of Oxford Brookes University staff found that for the majority (84%) of the respondents WLB is very essential for their career. Furthermore, the lack of awareness about WLB policies was

		identified as the major hindrance faced by employees in achieving WLB.
45	(Department of Labour Wellington New Zealand, 2004) Wellington, New Zealand	Both work and life are inseparable in nature. WLB is primarily the responsibility of individuals themselves. Because of the individualistic nature of the WLB, WLB means different to different people.
46	(Frone M. R., Work-family balance, 2003) Washington, U.S.A.	Defined work-family balance as a trade-off between work and non-work domains of the life rather than work and the life domain. The work-family balance construct which is of bidirectional both in its nature and effect. It is bidirectional in nature as it has work-to-family direction at the same time it is also bidirectional in effect as includes conflict as well as facilitation.
47	(Greenhaus & Allen, 2002) Washington, U.S.A.	Because of the multiplicity of definitions together with the absence of conscious among researchers with regard to the content and scope of the work-life balance concept, the term WFB and WLB become elusive. WLB is a concept that encompasses the concept of WFB.
48	(Kodz, Harper, & Dench, 2002) Brighton, U.K.	The authors coined the WLB take up gap. Where the employees are not willing to make use of policies and programmes offered by the employer because of its subsequent impact on their career, earnings, lack of knowledge, incompatible organisational culture and lack of access to infrastructure. Beyond this, support from the part of the supervisors and managers were also prevent employees from making use of available policies.
49	(Carnegie, 1986)	According to the author the happiness, as well as balance, should be traced by the individuals themselves through understanding their needs and wants rather than calling for help from others.

References

Alboher, M. (2012). *One Persion Multiple Careers.* New York: Warner Business Books.

Banker, A. K. (2012). *The Valmiki Syndrome Finding the work-life balance.* Noida: Random House India.

Blates, B. B., Clark, M. A., & Chakrabarti, M. (2010). Work-Life Blance: The Roles of Work-Family Conflict and Work-Family Facilitation. In *Oxford Handbook of Positive Psyhology* (pp. 201-2100). N.Y: Oxford University Press.

Bloom, N., Kretschmer, T., & Reenen, J. V. (2006). *Work-Life Balance, Management Practices and Productivity.* London: The London School of Economics and Political Science.

Carlson, D. S., Kacmar, K. M., Grzywacz, J. G., Tepper, B., & Whitten, D. (2013). *Work-Family Balance and Supervisor Appraised Citizenship Behavior: The Link of Positive Affect.* Institute of Behavioral and Applied Management.

Carnegie, D. (1986). *How to Enjoy Your Life and Your Job.* New York: Pocket Books.

Chandaria, I. B. (2013). *Work life balance – A study of dual career couples in medical sector.* Mumbai: Ishita Bharat Chandaria.

Chang, A., McDonald, P., & Burton, P. (2009). *Methodological choices in work-life balance research 1987 to 2006 : a critical review.* Queensland: Taylor & Francis.

Crawford, J. E. (2016). *Live Free Or Diy.* Redwood Digital Publishing.

Department of Labour New Zealand. (2006). *Work-Life Balance in New Zealand: A snapshot of employee and employer attitudes and experiences.* Wellington: Department of Labour.

Department of Labour Wellington New Zealand. (2004). *Achieving Balanced Livesand Employment; What New Zealanders are Saying about Work-Life Balance.* Wellington: Department of Labour Wellington New Zealand.

Dewe, P. J., O'Driscoll, M. P., & Cooper, C. L. (2010). *Coping with Work Stress A Review and Critique.* Malden: John Wiley & Sons Ltd.

Employment Market Analysis and Research. (2011). *The Third Work-Life Balance Employee Survey: Technical report.* Victoria Street: Department for Business, Innovation & Skills.

England, A. D. (2009). *The Essential Guide to Handling Workplace Harassment & Discrimination* (1st ed.). (L. Guerin, Ed.) California, United States OF America: Nolo.

Eurofound 2012. (2012). *Working time and work–life balance in a life course perspective.* Dublin: Eurofound.

Fleenor, J. W. (2004). Book Reviewing as an Important Scholarly Activity. (R. G. Jones, & L. Summers, Eds.) *Personal Psychology*, 1035-1037.

Frone, M. R. (2003). Work-family balance. In *Handbook of occupational health psychology* (pp. 143-162). Washington: American Psychological Association.

Furnham, A. (2013). *The Resilient Manager.* New York: Palgrave Macmillan. doi:10.1057/9781137361073

Gora, S. (2015). *Know Your Self for Better Work-Life Balance.* Mumbai: BecomeShakespeare.com.

Greenberg, C. L., & Avigdor, B. S. (2009). *What Happy Working Mothers Know.* New Jersey: John Wiley & Sons, Inc.

Greenhaus, J. H., & Brummelhuis, L. L. (2013). Models and frameworks underlying work–life research. In *Handbook of work–life integration among professionals* (p. 1434).

Gregory, A., & Milner, S. (2011). Fathers and work-life balance in France and the UK : policy and practice. 1-20. doi:10.1108/01443331111104797

Haddon, B., Hede, A., & Whiteoak, J. (2009). Work-Life Balance: Towards an Integrated Conceptual Framework.

Hutcheson, P. G. (2012). *Work-Life Balance.* Georgia: IEEE-USA.

International Labour Organisation. (2011). *Work–life balance.* Geneva: ILO.

Kelly, M. (2011). *Off Balance Getting Beyond the Work-Life Balance Myth to Personal and Professional Satisfaction.* New York: Hudson Street Press.

Kodz, J., Harper, H., & Dench, S. (2002). *Work-Life Balance: Beyond the Rhetoric.* Brighton: The Institute for Employment Studies. Retrieved from http://www.employment-studies.co.uk

Krings, B.-J., Nierling, L., Pedaci, M., & Piersanti, M. (2009). *Working time, gender and work-life balance.* Luxembourg: Europian Commission.

Lewis, S., & Beauregard, T. A. (2018). The Meanings of Work-Life Balance: A cultural perspective . In *The Cambridge handbook of the global work-family interface* (pp. 720-732). Cambridge: Cambridge University Press.

Littig, B. (2008). Work Life Balance – catchword or catalyst for sustainable work? *Reihe Soziologie / Sociological Series 85* , 1-14. Retrieved from http://www.ihs.ac.at

Maxwell, G. (2008). *Case Study Series on Work-Life Balance in Large Organizations.* Alexandria: Society for Human Resource Management.

Nomaguchi, K., & Milkie, M. A. (2011). *Gender, Beliefs about Spouse's Work-Family Conflict, and Relationship Quality.* Bowling : Bowling Green State University.

Oxford Brookes University. (2004). *Work-Life Balance: An audit of staff experience at Oxford Brookes University.* Wheatley: The Centre for Diversity Policy Research, Oxford Brookes University.

Poelmans, S., Odle-Dusseau, H. N., & Beham, B. (2008). Work-life balance: Individual and organizational strategies and practices. In *The Oxford Handbook of Organizational Well Being* (pp. 180-213). Oxford University Press.

Rantanen, J., Kinnunen, U., Mauno, S., & Tillemann, K. (2011). Introducing Theoretical Approaches to Work-Life Balance and Testing a New Typology Among Professionals. In S. Kaiser, M. Ringlstetter, D. Eikhof, & M. P. Cunha, *Creating Balance? International Prespectives on the Work-Life Integration of Professionals* (pp. 27-46). Berlin: Springer.

Ratna, R., Gupta, N., Devani, K., & Chawla, S. (2011, November). Work-Life Balance in BPO Sector. *International Journal of Physical and Social Science, 1*(3), 79-107. Retrieved from http://www.ijmra.us

Redmond, J., Valiulis, M., & Drew, E. (2006). *Literature review of issues related to work-life balance, workplace culture and maternity/childcare issues.* Dublin: Crisis Pregnancy Agency.

Reindl, C. U., Kaiser, S., & Stolz, M. L. (2011). Integrating Professional Work and Life: Conditions, Outcomes and Resources. In S. Kaiser, M. J. Ringlstetter, D. R. Eikhof, & M. P. Cunha (Eds.), *Creating Balance?* (pp. 3-26). London: Springer. doi:10.1007/978-3-642-16199-5

Schwingshackl, A. (2014). The Fallacy of Chasing after Work-Life Balance. In J. H. Lee, *Frontiers in Pediatrics* (pp. 1-3). Frontiers.

Shein, J., & Chen, C. P. (2011). *Work-Family Enrichment A Research of Positive Transfer.* Rotterdam: Sense Publishers.

Smithson, J., & Stokoe, E. H. (2005). Discourses of Work–Life Balance: Negotiating 'Genderblind' Terms in Organizations. In *Gender, Work and Organization* (pp. 147-168). Malden: Blackwell Publishing Ltd.

State Services Commission New Zealand . (2005). *Work-Life Balance: a resource for the State Services.* State Services Commission New Zealand: Wellington .

Tamsett, J. (2015). The Ultimate Guide to Work/Life Balance. *Optimum Health Magazine* . Analee Matthews.

Taylor, R. (2010). The Future of Work-Life Balance. *An ESRC Future of Work Programme Seminar Serie* (pp. 1-21). Swindon: E.E.R.C Economic and Social Research Council.

Thompson, C. (2006). *Under Pressure: Implication of Work-Family Conflict and Job Stress.* Toronto: Human Solutions.

Trindade, H. (2016). *How to Manage Stress with Self-Awareness.* (G. Bichard, Ed.) Hilton Trindade.

Visser, F., & Williams, L. (2006). *Work-Life Balance: Rhetoric Versus Reality.* London: The Work Foundation.

Vlems, E. (2005). *Work-Life Balance.* Geel: Katholieke Hogeschool Kempen.

Yuile, C., Chang, A., & Gudmundsson, A. (2005). Life friendly policies:Do they really help? In Fisher, & R. Huges, *Engaging the Multiple Contexts of*

Management: Convergence and Divergence of Management Theory and Practice: Proceedings of the 19th ANZAM Conference (pp. 1-12). Canaberra: Queensland University of Technology.

CHAPTER – 6

WORK-LIFE BALANCE – THE IMPEDING THOUGHTS

"We philosophers are mistake specialists. (I know, it sounds like a bad joke, but hear me out.) While other disciplines specialize in getting the right answers to their defining questions, we philosophers specialize in all the ways there are of getting things so mixed up, so deeply wrong, that nobody is even sure what the right questions are, let alone the answers. Asking the wrongs questions risks setting any inquiry off on the wrong foot. Whenever that happens, this is a job for philosophers! Philosophy - in every field of inquiry - is what you have to do until you figure out what questions you should have been asking in the first place."

– *Daniel Dennett (Philosopher)*

The concept of Work-life balance was instigated during the mid of 20th century. Feminization of the workforce and globalization where the two revolutionary change that take place during the era that have the potential to influence the working environment as well as work-life balance. Feminization of the workforce add fuel to the wide spared expansion of the work-life balance concept (Naithani, 2010). However, work-life balance studies become popular in the academic world only in the 21st century. The theory of role conflict proposed by Greenhaus and Beutell in 1985 can be recognised as the first legitimate enquiry into the field of work-life balance research. It was actually this particular work of Greenhaus and Beutell that gives a conceptual and theoretical basis to the concept of work-life balance. Boarder theory introduced by Clark 2000 have alley with the role theory with regard to inter-role relations. Although till now there were no theoretically sound and commonly accepted single definition for work-life balance.

6.1 Obscurities Over the Work-Life Balance Concept and Scope

With regard to work-life balance, a number of ambiguities are there. The term work-life balance itself is a subject matter of debate. The concept of work-life balance itself is wrong as the work is the part of our day to day life and the problem of work-life balance arise only when segregate the work form his life and view it separately (Kelly, 2011). Similarly, work-life balance, work to non-work balance and work to family balance were used interchangeably; which is another subject of debate. Another ambiguity is with regard to the meaning as well as ascertainment of the work-life balance. The early concept of work-life balance is about segmentation, where there is no relationship between various domains of life. But this concept does not acquire any attention. Work-life balance is the absence or minimal of inter-role conflict (Greenhaus & Beutell, 1985). Whereas (Clark, 2000) defines work-life balance as satisfaction with regard to various roles in life. Similarly, work-life balance is defined as the situation at which there is minimal inter-role conflict and maximum inter-role facilitation (Frone, 2003; Grzywacz & Bass, 2003; Hayman, 2005).

Furthermore, there here exists the absence of researcher's conscience over content and scope of work-life balance concept (e.g., Casper, Vaziri, Wayne, DeHauw, & Greenhaus, 2017; Brough, et al., 2014; Kalliath & Brough, 2008). Later in 2008 Kalliath and Brough came up with a new definition for work-life balance where the work-life balance is theorised as individual perception about inter-role silence. Again in 2009 Carlson, Grzywacz, and Zivnuska put forward an innovative conceptualisation to the work-family balance concept. They conceptualised work-family balance as the fulfilment of family and work role expectations. The model of Kalliath and Brough were empirically validated by Brougha, et al., in the year 2014. The major drawback of this particular model is that it enquires about personal life perceptions in a general sense.

There is a need to define the content of the 'life or non-work' domain explicitly. The absence of conscience over content scope with regard to 'life domain' often cordon the objective assessment of the work-life balance. This is because the meaning of 'life' is a subjective concept and is dependent on the individual/employee himself. While defining 'work-life balance' it's crucial to fence the content scope of the 'life' domain; so, that an objective assessment would be possible. Unfortunately, in the realm of work-life balance research, the 'life' or 'non-work' domain is defined vaguely rather than specifically. The ambiguity in defining the content scope of 'life' or 'non-work' domain, annihilate the potential of the research to draw an accurate assessment of respondent's work-life balance as the researcher is inept in comprehending the 'exact' meaning that the respondent conceived.

The conceptual and empirical underpinning between conflict, enrichment and balance remain underexplored. The interrelationship among these constructs needs to be estimated for defining the construct of work-life balance unanimously. The theoretical distinction among positive spillover, facilitation, enrichment and, enhancement need to be validated empirically. Similarly, the theoretical distinction among negative spillover, conflict, and interference also need to be validated empirically. The researchers have established the conceptual independence between the aforesaid constructs. Whereas, the empirical validation of the conceptual independence remains unexplored. Family and work support is positively associated with work-life balance and work-family enrichment. Whereas lack of support mechanism and facilitative policies at work and organisational was positively related to work family conflict and negatively related to work-family balance (Allen, Herst, Bruck, & Sttton, 2000). Although Shein and Chen (2011), has identified the presence of conflict as well as enrichment simoultaneously in individuals. Furthermore, because of the jingle-jungle fallacy (see The Jingle-Jangle fallacy of Work–Nonwork Balance: A Comprehensive and Meta-Analytic Review of Its Meaning and Measurement by Casper, Vaziri, Wayne, DeHauw, & Greenhaus, 2017 for details), work-life balance researchers often failed to explore the work-life balance level of the employees.

6.2 Personal Psychology, Cognitive Capability, and Work-life Balance

The word personality is derived from the Latin word 'persona' which in turn means 'mask'. That is personality is the mask that the individuals present before others (Sociology Guide.Com, 2016). The personality is a system of parts that is organised, develops, and is expressed in a person's actions. Whereas system parts indicate motives, emotions, mental model and the self (Mayer, 2007). Studies have identified the relationship between personality and work-life balance. However, most of such studies followed an exploratory design to towel some insights into the relationship between personality and work-life balance. Several researchers (Moshoeu, 2017; Poulose & Sudarsan, 2014; Kundnani & Mehta, 2014; Devadoss & Minnie, 2013; Kaur, 2013) acclaimed that the personality inclination of work-life balance needs to be explored in detail. Studies often identified the relationship between certain personality types and their association with work-life balance. Personality type is only one of several types of personality classification.

With regard to the personality inclination of work-life balance, the existing literature has a significant dearth in predicting the extent of the effect that each of personality characteristics has on employee work-life balance. The researchers have explored the relationship between personality and work-life balance, but the researchers were often cornered towards certain characteristics. Furthermore, the personal psychology of the employee seems to be a potential intervening variable between work-life balance and socio-cultural demographics and/ characteristics (work, family, personal and societal), as the socio-cultural demographics not only have relationship with employee work-life balance but also with the personal psychology of the employee.

Research exploring the relationship between individual difference (personality traits) and work-family balance were limited (Michel, Clark, & Beiler, Work–life conflict and its effects, 2013; see also Eby, Casper, Lockwood, Bordeaux, & Brinley, 2005). There is a need to identify the relationship between individual difference e.g., personality, role silence, attitude, belief, and values) and work-life related constructs (Michel, Clark,

& Beiler, 2013). Therefore, the intervening effect of cognitive resources between work-life balance and socio-cultural demographics and/ characteristics to be explored further. Studies often found that there's a relationship between cognitive capability and work-life balance. However, the studies failed to assess the predictive capability of psychological characteristics to prognosticate work-life balance.

6.3 Psycho-Social Blend of the Work-Life Balance Concept

Until recently work-life balance is studied either from a socio-cultural perspective or from a psychological perspective. The psycho-social perspective of work-life balance is of recent origin. It was Casper, Vaziri, Wayne, DeHauw, and Greenhaus in the year 2017 proposed a theoretically well-grounded definition for work-life balance that validated it psycho-social blend. Casper, Vaziri, Wayne, DeHauw, & Greenhaus (2017) delineates work-life balance as a psycho-social construct and proclaims that the psycho-social characteristics and resource base of an individual and defines the work-life balance level of an employee. Martin (2016) proposed a new model of work-life balance based on intelligence and egalitarianism. Intelligence is a cognitive resource whereas egalitarianism is cultural characteristics. That is, Martin's model of work-life balance also validates the psycho-social intermingling of work-life balance construct. Though, there was ambiguity regarding the direction and path of relationship in between; the psycho-social intermingling of work-life balance construct is a fact that can't be denied.

Therefore, the work-life balance being a psycho-social construct work-life balance need to be addressed from a psycho-social perspective. That is, the relationship between WLB, psychological characteristic, socio-cultural demographics, socio-cultural resources, work demographics, and work resources should be studied together. Awkwardly, researchers often explored work-life balance either form socio-cultural perspective or from a psychological perspective. That is, the holistic view (psycho-social perspective) of work-life balance remained underexplored, resulting handicapped view about work-life balance. Therefore, there is a need to explore work-life balance from a psycho-social perspective.

6.4 Socio-Cultural Factors and Work-Life Balance: The Discrepancies

Studies (Dhanya & Kinslin, 2017; Sav, 2016; Farkiya, 2015; Poulose & Sudarsan, 2014) identified that work-life balance has a relationship with socio-cultural demographics and characteristics of an employee. Likewise, Personal demographics were also found to have a relationship with employee work-life balance level. Demographic characteristics such as age, gender, human generation, and other features have the ability to differentiate work-life balance in between (Rosanna, 2012; Parker, Albany, & Citera, 2010; Sonia, 2012; Sunderaraj, 2012; Vanishree, 2012; Walia, 2011). However, there were also studies that cited the invariability of the work-life balance with regard to demographic variables (Frone, Russell, & Cooper, 1992; Ajay KR & Amanjot, 2012). Family-related variables such as the number of children, family type, family support, carer responsibility have relationship with work-life balance (Dewe, O'Driscoll, & Cooper, 2010; Rantanen, Kinnunen, MaunO, & Tillemann, 2010). This indicates ambiguity with regard to this. That is, albeit findings with regard to the relationship between socio-cultural factors and work-life balance were contradictory in nature as the researchers failed to validate the identified relationship both cross-sectionally as well as longitudinally.

The socio-cultural intermingling of the work-life balance, questions the validity of a universal definition of work-life balance. Socio-cultural factors are geographical bound. There exists wide disparity among people across the different socio-cultural background. Each cultural/ethnic group has its own views, traditions, customs, and beliefs. That is, the work-life balance being a construct that has intermingling with socio-cultural factors, its meaning, importance, and influence will be different depending upon the socio-cultural characteristics. The finding of the Kurowska (2018), that the egalitarian as a factor that has the dominant influence of the employee work-life balance level can be read jointly and requires further inquiry with this regard. That is, the meaning, importance, and influence of work-life balance on the employee with reference to the socio-cultural characteristics.

6.5 Work-Life Balance as an Intervening Construct

Work-life balance is an upshot construct when it is compared with socio-cultural demographics, characteristics, and cognitive resources. Whereas, work-life balance is an explanatory variable for various domain related upshot constructs such as life satisfaction, work satisfaction, family satisfaction, happiness, turnover intention etc., Studies have found that the work-life balance has the potential to influence job satisfaction, life satisfaction, employee turnover, and family satisfaction (Li, 2018; Ganiyu, Fields, & Atiku, 2017; Brough, Siu, O'Driscoll, & Timmis, 2015; Farkiya, 2015; Poulose & Sudarsan, 2014; Shree, 2013); likewise, studies also have found that various work, family, socio-cultural and cognitive characteristics as well as qualities have relationship with employee work-life balance (Abdullah, Aremu, & Abogunrin, 2018; Jones, 2018; Kurowska, 2018; Prithi & Vasumathi, 2018). That is, the work-life balance has the potential to interpose the relationship between environmental characteristic/factors and various domain related upshot constructs. Hence, the intervening effect of work-life balance between socio-cultural characteristics and various domain related upshot constructs need to be examined further as there's a paucity of studies exploring the aforesaid relationship.

6.6 Marginalisation of the Work-Life Balance Research

The feminisation of the work environment is often identified as the root cause responsible for the development of the work-life balance concept. The feminisation of work environment resulted in the dismantlement of the gender role divide prevailed in the society. Because of the work role reorganisation among gender, work-life balance has become inevitable not only work working women but also for working men too. Unfortunately, the work-life balance research ignored the work-life balance need of men and conceptualised work-life balance as a concept pertaining to working women alone. Out of 274 works reviewed, 97 of the works exclusively examined the work-life balance with reference to women and only nominal works (3 out of 274) exclusively examined the work-life balance with reference to men. That is, the work-life balance research often overlooks the work-life balance need of men/fathers. Therefore, researchers should explore work-life balance from a gender-neutral perspective rather than from the traditional gendered frame.

Another important shortfall with regard to the work-life balance research is that the work-life balance research ignored the work-life balance need of marginalised (ethnic minorities, disabled people, un-organised labours, etc.,) sections in the society, especially the disabled. Because of their physical incapability, the disabled are supposed to have greater difficulty in balancing professional demand and personal demands. To the paradox, the work-life balance research ignored the work-life balance need of disabled employees. The work-life balance being a concept build upon the widespread recognition of enlightenment and humanitarian values, the work-life balance need of the marginalised sections need to be engrossed deprived of any postponement.

References

Abdullah, A. S., Aremu, N. S., & Abogunrin, A. P. (2018). Work-Life Balance and Academic Staff Performance in Nigerian Universities. *Ilorin Journal of Human Resource Management*, 102-113.

Allen, T. D., Herst, D. E., Bruck, C. S., & Sttton, M. (2000). Consequences Associated With Work-to-Family Conflict:A Review and Agenda for Future Research. *Journal of Occupational Health Psychology, 5*(2), 278-308. doi:10.1037//1076-8998.5.2.278

Bansal, A. K., & Raj, L. (2017). A Study on Work Life Balance of Women Employees in Indian Oil Corporation Limited Mathura (U.P .). *CPUH-Research Journal*, 6-11. Retrieved from http://www.cpuh.in/academics/academic_journals.php

Barge, G. C. (2011). *A Phenomenological Study of Competing Priorities and African American Women Striving to Achieve Work-Life Balance.* Ph.D Thesis.

Brough, P., Siu, O. L., O'Driscoll, M., & Timmis, C. (2015). Work–family enrichment and satisfaction: The mediating role of self-efficacy and work–life balance . *The International Journal of Human Resource Management*. doi:10.1080/09585192.2015.1075574

Brough, P., Timmsb, C., O'Driscollc, M. P., Kalliathd, T., Siue, O.-L., Sitf, C., & Log, D. (2014, March). Work–life balance: a longitudinal evaluation of a new measure across Australia and New Zealand workers. *The International Journal of Human Resource Management, 25*(19), 2724-2744. doi:10.1080/09585192.2014.899262

Carlson, D. S., Grzywacz, J. G., & Zivnuska, S. (2009, October). Is work–family balance more than conflict and enrichment? *National Institute of Health, 62*(10), 1-20. doi:10.1177/0018726709336500

Casper, W. J., Vaziri, H., Wayne, J. H., DeHauw, S., & Greenhaus, J. (2017). The Jingle-Jangle of Work–Nonwork Balance: A Comprehensive and Meta-Analytic Review of Its Meaning and Measurement. *Journal of Applied Psychology*. doi:10.1037/apl0000259

Clark, S. C. (2000). Work/Family Border Theory: A New Theory of Work/Family Balance. *Human Relations*, 747-770. doi:10.1177/0018726700536001

Devadoss, A., & Minnie, J. B. (2013). A Study of Personality Influence in Building Work Life Balance Using Fuzzy Relation Mapping (FRM). *International Journal of Data Mining Techniques and Applications*, 211-216.

Dhanya, J., & Kinslin, D. (2017, January 30). *A study on work life balance of women employees at ULCCS Ltd, Kozhkode*. Retrieved from Resrarchgate.net: https://www.researchgate.net/publication

Farkiya, R. (2015). *A Study of Work Life Balance in Health Care Industry.* PhD Thesis, Indore.

Frone, M. R. (2003). Work-family balance. In *Handbook of occupational health psychology* (pp. 143-162). Washington: American Psychological Association.

Ganiyu, I., Fields, Z., & Atiku, S. (2017). Work-life balance strategies, work-family satisfaction and employees' job performance in Lagos, Nigeria's manufacturing sector. *Journal of Contemporary Management*, 441-460.

Greenhaus, J. H., & Beutell, N. J. (1985). Sources of Conflict between Work and Family Roles. *The Academy of Management Review, 10*(1), 76-88. Retrieved April 8, 2016, from http://www.jstor.org/stable/258214

Grzywacz, J. G., & Bass, B. L. (2003). Work, family, and mental health: Testing different models of work-family fit. *Journal of Marriage and Family*, 248-261.

Hayman, J. (2005). Psychometric Assessment of an Instrument Designed to Measure Work Life Balance. *Research and Practice in Human Resource Management, 13*(1), 85-91.

Jones, K. (2018). *Work-Life Balance: Organizational Leadership and Individual Strategies among Successful Women Real Estate Brokers.* Ph.D, Pepperdine University , Graduate School of Education and Psychology.

Kalliath, T., & Brough, P. (2008). Work–life balance: A review of the meaning of the balance construct. *Journal of Management & Organization , 14*(3), 323-327.

Kaur, J. (2013). WORK-LIFE BALANCE: ITS CORRELATION WITH SATISFACTION WITH LIFE AND PERSONALITY DIMENSIONS AMONGST COLLEGE TEACHERS. *International Journal of Marketing, Financial Services & Management Research, 8*(2), 24-35. Retrieved from www.indianresearchjournals.com

Kelly, M. (2011). *Off Balance Getting Beyond the Work-Life Balance Myth to Personal and Professional Satisfaction.* New York: Hudson Street Press.

Kundnani, N., & Mehta, P. (2014). Role of Personality Traits in Work-Life Balance. *International Journal of Management Research & Review*, 722-731.

Kurowska, A. (2018). Gendered Effects of Home-Based Work on Parents' Capability to Balance Work with Non-work: Two Countries with Different Models of Division of Labour Compared. *Social Indicators Research*. doi:10.1007/s11205-018-2034-9

Li, Y. (2018). Effects of Work-Life Balance on Organizational Commitment: A Study in China's State-Owned Enterprise. *World Journal of Social Science Research*, 144-166. doi:10.22158/wjssr.v5n2p144

Martin, L. K. (2016). *Norway Leads the World in Gender Equality and Work-Life Balance: A Qualitative Life Course Study of Norwegian Women.* Ph.D Thesis.

Mayer, J. D. (2007). Asserting the Definition of Personality. *The Online Newsletter for Personality Science*, (pp. 1-4).

Michel, J. S., Clark, M. A., & Beiler, A. A. (2013). Work–life conflict and its effects. In *Handbook of work–life integration among professionals* (pp. 58-76).

Moshoeu, A. N. (2017). *A Model of Personality Traits and Work-Life Balance As Determinants of Employee Engangement.* University of South Africa. Abigail Ngokwana Moshoeu.

Naithani, P. (2010). Overview of Work-Life Balance Discourse and Its Relevance in Current Economic Scenario. *Asian Social Science*, 148-155. Retrieved from www.ccsenet.org/ass

Poulose, S., & Sudarsan, N. (2014). Work Life Balance: A Conceptual Review. *International Journal of Advances in Management and Economics, 3*(2), 1-17. Retrieved from www.managementjournal.info

Prithi, S., & Vasumathi, A. (2018). The Influence of Demographic Profile on Work Life Balance of Women Employees in Tannery Industry – An Empirical Study. *Pertanika J. Soc. Sci. & Hum*, 259-284.

Rothberg, S. (2014). *The Journey of Female Cancer Patients or Survivors while Striving for Personal Work-life Balance .* ProQuest LLC.

Russo, M., Shteigman, A., & Carmeli, A. (2015). Workplace and family support and work–life balance: Implications for individual psychological availability and energy at work. *The Journal of Positive Psychology*, 173-188. doi:10.1080/17439760.2015.1025424

Sav, A. (2016). The role of religion in work-life interface. *The International Journal of Human Resource Management*. doi:10.1080/09585192.2016.1255905

Shahisaman, L. (2015). *A Phenomenological Study of Women in India Striving to Achieve Work-Life Balance in Finance with Competing Priorities.* Ann Arbor: ProQuest.

Shein, J., & Chen, C. P. (2011). *Work-Family Enrichment A Research of Positive Transfer.* Rotterdam: Sense Publishers.

Shree, R. M. (2013). *A Study on Worklife Balance and Life Satisfaction of Critical Care Nurses at Coimbatore District.* Bharathiar University, Coimbatore.

Sociology Guide.Com. (2016). *Personality*. Retrieved from Sociology Guide.

Toston, S. (2014). *Work-life Balance Straegies of Women Leaders within the Church of God in Christ.* Ann Arbor: ProQuest LLC.

Triplett, J. (2016). *The Work-Life Balance of Female Adjunct Faculty at Southern California Community Colleges.* Ann Arbor: ProQuest LLC.

Bibliography

Abdullah, A. S., Aremu, N. S., & Abogunrin, A. P. (2018). Work-Life Balance and Academic Staff Performance in Nigerian Universities. *Ilorin Journal of Human Resource Management*, 102-113.

Abe, E. N., Fields, Z., & Abe, I. I. (2016). The Efficacy of Wellness Programmes as Work-Life Balance Strategies in the South African Public Service . *Journal of Economics and Behavioral Studies, 8*(6), 52-67.

Abele, A. E., & Volmer, J. (2011). Dual-Career Couples: Specific Challenges for Work-Life Integration. In S. Kaiser, M. J. Ringlstetter, D. R. Eikhof, & M. P. Cunha, *Creating Balance?* (pp. 173-192). Heidelberg: Springer.

Ability Magazine. (2018). *Managing Work, Life, and Disability*. Retrieved from Ability Magazine: https://abilitymagazine.com/Balancing-disability.html

Abubaker, M. A. (2015). *Work Life Balance Policies and Practices: Case studies of the Palestinian Telecommunication Sector.* University of Bradford. Bradford: University of Bradford.

Acas. (2015). *Flexible Working and Work-life Balance.* Acas.

Agosti, M. T., Bringsén, Å., & Andersson, I. (2017). The complexity of resources related to work-life balance and well-being – a survey among municipality employees in Sweden. *The International Journal of Human Resource Management*, 2351-2374. doi:10.1080/09585192.2017.1340323

Ajay K.R, S., & Amanjot, S. (2012). Work Life Balance and Subjective Well Being: A Comparative Study in Public and Private Institutes in Higher Education.

Albertsen, K., Rafnsdóttir, G. L., Grimsmo, A., Tómasson, K., & Kauppinen, K. (2008). Workhours and worklife balance. *SJWEH Suppl*, 14-21.

Alboher, M. (2012). *One Persion Multiple Careers.* New York: Warner Business Books.

Alkhatib, A. J. (2013, October 13). *Would you discourage to cite PhD theses?* Retrieved from ResearchGate: https://www.researchgate.net/

Allen, T. D., Herst, D. E., Bruck, C. S., & Sttton, M. (2000). Consequences Associated With Work-to-Family Conflict:A Review and Agenda for Future Research. *Journal of Occupational Health Psychology, 5*(2), 278-308. doi:10.1037//1076-8998.5.2.278

Amber, T., Hassan, D. A., Anam, S., & Asif, T. (2012, January). Work-Life Balance as a best practice Model of Human Rerource Management: A Win Win Situational Tool for the Employees and Organisations. *Mediterranean Journal of Social Sciences, 3*(1), 577-584. doi:10.5901/mjss.2012.03.01.577

Andrea R. Beyer, M. i., Fasolo, B., Graeff, P. d., & Hillege, H. (2015). Risk attitudes and personality traits predict perceptions of benefits and risks for medicinal products: a field study of European medical assessors. *Value in Health*, 91-99. doi:10.1016/j.jval.2014.10.011

Andysz, A., Najder, A., & Merecz-Kot, D. (2014). Organizational and individual determinants of using initiatives conducive to successful work-life balance. *MED-PR*, 119-129.

Anghel, R. G. (2011). From irregular migrants to fellow Europeans: Changes in Romanian migratory flows. In M. Bommes, & G. Sciortino, *Foggy Social Structures Irregular Migration, European Labour Markets and the Welfare State* (pp. 23-44). Amsterdam : Amsterdam University Press.

Antai, D., Oke, A., Braithwaite, P., & Anthony, D. (2015). A 'Balanced' Life: WorkLife Balance and Sickness Absence in Four Nordic Countries. *Int J Occup Environ Med, 6*(4), 205-222. Retrieved from www.theijoem.com

Areepattamannil, S., & Hashim, J. (2017). The questionnaire for Eudaimonic well-being (QEWB): Psychometric properties in a non-western adolescent sample. *Personality and Individual Differences*, 236-241.

Armasu, L. (2017, December 2). *Top 25 Cryptocurrencies By Market Cap*. Retrieved from Tomshardware: http://www.tomshardware.com/picturestory/778-biggest-cryptocurrencies.html

Aryee, S., Srinivas, E. S., & Hwee, H. (2005). Rhythms of Life: Antecedents and Outcomes of Work-Family Balance in Employed Parents. *Journal of Applied Psychology, 90*(1), 132-138.

Asendorpf, J. B. (2009). Personality: traits and situations. In P. J. Corr, & G. Matthews (Eds.), *The Cambridge Handbook of Personality Psychology* (pp. 43-53). Cambridge: Cambridge University Press.

Atheya, R., & Arora, R. (2013). Work-Life Balance (WLB); A Cause of Concern in Banking Sector. *International Journal of Research in Commerce, Economics & Management*, 42-46.

Ayudhya, U. C., Prouska, R., & Beauregard, A. (2017). The Impact of Global Economic Crisis and Austerity on Quality of Working Life and Work-LifeBalance:ACapabilitiesPerspective. *European Management Review*. doi:10.1111/emre.12128

Azeem, S. M., & Akhtar, N. (2014). The Influence of Work Life Balance and Job Satisfaction on Organizational Commitment of Healthcare Employees. *International Journal of Human Resource Studies, 4*(2), 18-24. doi:10.5296/ijhrs.v4i2.5667

Baltimore County Public Schools. (2017). *Planning the Introduction - Explaining the Significance of the Problem*. Retrieved from Develop a Research Proposal: https://www.bcps.org

Bandura, A. (1999). Social Cognitive Theory of Personality. In *Handbook of personality* (pp. 154-196). New York: Guilford Publications.

Banker, A. K. (2012). *The Valmiki Syndrome Finding the work-life balance.* Noida: Random House India.

Bansal, A. K., & Raj, L. (2017). A Study on Work Life Balance of Women Employees in Indian Oil Corporation Limited Mathura (U.P .). *CPUH-Research Journal*, 6-11. Retrieved from http://www.cpuh.in/academics/academic_journals.php

Banu, A. R. (2015). A Structural Equation Model-I for Work-Life Balance of IT professionals in Chennai. *European Journal of Business and Management, 7*(4), 221-229. Retrieved from www.iiste.org

Banu, A. R., & Duraipandian, K. (2014). Development of an Insrument to measure Work Life Balance of IT Professionals in Chennai. *International Journal of Management, 5*(11), 21-31. Retrieved from http://www.iaeme.com/IJM.asp

Barb Clews & Associates. (n.d.). *Work and Personal Life Balance.* Retrieved from Barb Clews: www.barbclews.com

Barge, G. C. (2011). *A Phenomenological Study of Competing Priorities and African American Women Striving to Achieve Work-Life Balance.* Ph.D Thesis.

Barling, J. (1986). Interrole conflict and marital functioning amongst employed fathers. *Journal of Organizational Behavior*, 61-66. doi:10.1002/job.4030070108

Barrett, H. (2018, June 15). Employers baffled by dual-career couples with joint ambitions . *Financial Times*.

Barrow, L., & Bullock, I. (1996). *Democratic ideas and the British Labour movement, 1880-1914.* London: Cambridge University Press.

Barton, B., & Peat, J. (2014). *Medical Statistics A Guide to SPSS, Data Analysis and Critical Appraisal.* John Wiley & Sons Ltd.

Bashir, S. (2017, March 27). How to write Significance of Research. Shahid Bashir. Retrieved from https://www.youtube.com/watch?v=w3pkTB-13cU

Bauer, S. (2017). *Work-Life Balanced Culture, Work Flexibility, and Inducements: Impact on Perceived Organizational Attractiveness and Job Pursuit Intention.* Master Degree Thesis.

Beauregard, T. A., & Henry, L. C. (2007). Making the link between work-life balance practices and organizational performance. *Human resource management review*, 9-22. doi:10.1016/j.hrmr.2008.09.001

Beha, B., Drobnič, S., Präg, P., Baierl, A., & Eckner, J. (2018). Part-time work and gender inequality in Europe: a comparative analysis of satisfaction with work–life balance. *European Societies*. doi:10.1080/14616696.2018.1473627

Bell, A. S., Rajendran, D., & Theiler, S. (2012). Job Stress, Wellbeing, Work-Life Balance and Work-Life Conflict Among Australian Academics. *Electronic Journal of Applied Psychology*, 25-37.

Bellman, G. M. (1990). Balancing Your Work in Your Life. *Training and Development Journal* .

Bennett, B. (2012). *Logically Fallacious The Ultimate Collection of Over 300 Logical Fallacies.* Sudbury: Bo Bennett.

Berger, D., Fink, A., Gomez, M. M., & Unterrainer, H.-F. (2015). The Validation of a Spanish Version of the Multidimensional Inventory of Religious/Spiritual Well-Being in Mexican College Students. *The Spanish Journal of Psychology.*

Bhalla, A., & Kang, L. S. (2018). The Role of Personality in Influencing Work Family Balance Experience: A study of Indian Journals. *Global Business Review.* doi:10.1177/0972150918779157

Bharathy, A. (2012). A Perceptual Analysis of Employee Work Life Balance in ITES/BPO Sector. *South Asian Journal of Marketing and Management Research, 2*(7), 12-25. Retrieved from http://www.saarj.com

Bhardwaj, R. (2017, May 13). *Beyond Flexibility: How to make workplaces women friendly.* Retrieved from People Matters: https://www.peoplematters.in/blog/diversity/beyond-flexibility-how-to-make-workplaces-women-friendly-15434?utm_source=peoplematters&utm_medium=interstitial&utm_campaign=learnings-of-the-day

Bhasi, M., Renuka, V. V., & Rajkumar, S. (2017). A Study on Influence of Religion on Inheritance in Family Business. *Vilakshan: The XIMB Journal of Management*, 31-50.

Bhatia, S., Redpath, S. M., Suryawanshi, K., & Mishra, C. (2016). The Relationship Between Religion and Attitudes Toward Large Carnivores in Northern India? *Human Dimensions of Wildlife An International Journal.* doi:10.1080/10871209.2016.1220034

Blates, B. B., Clark, M. A., & Chakrabarti, M. (2010). Work-Life Blance: The Roles of Work-Family Conflict and Work-Family Facilitation. In *Oxford Handbook of Positive Psyhology* (pp. 201-2100). N.Y: Oxford University Press.

Bloom, N., Kretschmer, T., & Reenen, J. V. (2006). *Work-Life Balance, Management Practices and Productivity.* London: The London School of Economics and Political Science.

BLS Reports. (2014). *Women in the Labor Force: A Databook.* U.S. Bureau of Labour Statistics.

Bohlea, P., Quinlana, M., Kennedya, D., & Williamson, A. (2004). Working hours, work-life conflict and health in precarious and "permanent" employment. *XVI International Symposium on Night and Shiftwork, November 2003*, (pp. 19-25). Santos.

Bolívar, J., Daponte, A., Rodríguez, M., & Sánchez, J. J. (2010). The Influence of Individual, Social and Physical Environment Factors on Physical Activity in the Adult Population in Andalusia, Spain. *International Journal of Environmental Research and Public Health*, 60-77. doi:10.3390/ijerph7010060

Bonebright, C. A., Clay, D. L., & Ankenmann, R. D. (2000). The relationship of workaholism with work–life conflict, life satisfaction, and purpose in life. *Journal of Counseling Psychology, 47*(4), 469-477.

Bonga, A. (2017, November 14). *Guide: Understanding The Types Of Cryptocurrency Tokens*. Retrieved from Bitcoinhub: https://bitcoinhub.co.za/functions-cryptocurrency-tokens/

Boods, D. N., & Beile, P. (2005). Scholars before researchers: On the centrality of the dissertation literature review in research preparation. 3-15.

Booth, A. L., & Frank, J. (2005). Glender and work-Life Flexibility in the Labour Market. In D. M. Houston, *Work-Life Balance in the 21st Century* (pp. 11-28). Palgrave Macmillan: New York.

Boschman, J. S., Lundström, A. N., Nilsson, T., & Hagberg, J. K. (2017). Relationships between work-related factors and musculoskeletal health with current and future work ability among male workers. *International Archives of Occupational and Environmental Health*, 517-526. doi:10.100s/2Fs00420-017-1216-0

Boswell, W. R., & Olson-Buchanan, J. B. (2007). The Use of Communication Technologies After Hours: The Role of Work Attitudes and Work-Life Conflict. *Journal of Management*, 592-610. doi:10.1177/0149206307302552

Boyle, G. J. (2008). Critique of Five Factor Model of Personality. In *Humanities & Social Sciences papers.* Bond University.

Boyle, G. J., & Helmes, E. (2009). Methods of personality assessment. In P. J. Corr, & G. Matthews (Eds.), *The Cambridge Handbook of Personality Psychology* (pp. 110-126). Cambridge: Cambridge University Press.

Branch, S. (2008). *The Effects of Organisational Work-Life Balance Initiatives on Accountants in New Zealand.* University of Canterbury . anterbury : Sarah Branch.

Branett, R. C., & Hyde, J. S. (2001). Women, Men, Work and Family: An Expansionist Theory. *American Psychologist*, 781-796.

Braun, O. L. (2016). *Bitcoin and Cryptocurrency: A guide to Blockchain, Bitcoin and other Cryptocurrencies .*

Brough, P., Siu, O. L., O'Driscoll, M., & Timmis, C. (2015). Work–family enrichment and satisfaction: The mediating role of self-efficacy and work–life balance . *The International Journal of Human Resource Management*. doi:10.1080/09585192.2015.1075574

Brough, P., Timmsb, C., O'Driscollc, M. P., Kalliathd, T., Siue, O.-L., Sitf, C., & Log, D. (2014, March). Work–life balance: a longitudinal evaluation of a new measure across Australia and New Zealand workers. *The International Journal of Human Resource Management, 25*(19), 2724-2744. doi:10.1080/09585192.2014.899262

Brückner, M. (2013, September 21). *Would you discourage to cite PhD theses?* Retrieved from ResearchGate: https://www.researchgate.net/

Bruckner, M. (2013). On the Simultaneity Problem in the Aid and Growth Debate. *Journal of Applied Econometrics*, 126-150.

Bulger, C. A., Matthews, R. A., & Hoffman, M. E. (2007). Work and Personal Life Boundary Management: Boundary Strength, Work/Personal Life Balance, and the Segmentation–Integration Continuum. *Journal of Occupational Health Psychology*, 365-375. doi:10.1037/1076-8998.12.4.365

Bureau of Labor Statistics. (2018, April 19). *Employment Characteristics of Families Summary.* Bureau of Labor Statistics.

Burnett, K. (2011). Chapter - 2 People/ HR. In K. Burnett, *Practical Contact Center Collaboration* (p. 442). Pittsburgh: Ken Burnett.

Cameron, T. L. (2011). *The Professional & the Personal: Worklife Balance and Mid-Level Student Affairs Administrators.* Blacksburg: Tracey LaShawne Cameron.

Carey, D., & Trakulhun, S. (2009). Universalism, Diversity, and the Postcolonial Enlightenment. In D. Carey, & L. Festa, *Postcolonial Enlightenment* (pp. 243-277). Oxford: Oxford University Press.

Carlson, D. S., Grzywacz, J. G., & Zivnuska, S. (2009, October). Is work–family balance more than conflict and enrichment? *National Institute of Health, 62*(10), 1-20. doi:10.1177/0018726709336500

Carlson, D. S., Kacmar, K. M., & Williams, L. J. (2000). Construction and Initial Validation of a Multidimensional Measure of Work–Family Conflict. *Journal of Vocational Behavior, 56*, 249-276. doi:10.1006/jvbe.1999.1713

Carlson, D. S., Kacmar, K. M., Grzywacz, J. G., Tepper, B., & Whitten, D. (2013). *Work-Family Balance and Supervisor Appraised Citizenship Behavior: The Link of Positive Affect.* Institute of Behavioral and Applied Management.

Carlson, D. S., Kacmar, K. M., Wayne, J. H., & Grzywacz, J. G. (2006). Mesuring the positive side of the work-family interface: Development and validation of a work-family enrichment scale. *Journal of Vocational Behavior , 68*, 131-164. doi:10.1016/j.jvb.2005.02.002

Carmeli, A. (2003). The relationship between emotional intelligence and work attitudes, behavior. *Journal of Managerial Psychology, 18*(8), 788-813. doi:10.1108/02683940310511881

Carnegie, D. (1986). *How to Enjoy Your Life and Your Job.* New York: Pocket Books.

Casper, W. J., Vaziri, H., Wayne, J. H., DeHauw, S., & Greenhaus, J. (2017). The Jingle-Jangle of Work–Nonwork Balance: A Comprehensive and Meta-Analytic Review of Its Meaning and Measurement. *Journal of Applied Psychology.* doi:10.1037/apl0000259

Caughey, M. (2012). *Bitcoin Step by Step.* Kindle Edition.

Central Statistical Office Ministry of Statistics and Program Implementation Government of India. (2017). *Quatrely Estimate of Gross Domestic Product for the forth Quartrer (Q4) 2016-2017.* New Delhi: Central

Statistical Office Ministry of Statistics and Program Implementation Government of India.

Centre for Substance Abuse Treatment. (1999). Chapter 6-Brief Humanistic and Existential Therapies. In *Brief Interventions and Brief Therapies for Substance Abuse* (pp. 105-121). Rockville: Substance Abuse and Mental Health Services Administration.

Cervone, D., Shadel, W. G., & Jencius, S. (2001). Social-Cognitive Theory of Personality Assessment. *Personality and Social Psychology Review*, 33-51.

Chan, X. W., Kalliath, T., Brough, P., Siu, O.-L., O'Driscoll, M. P., & Timms, C. (2015). Work–family enrichment and satisfaction: the mediating role of self-efficacy and work–life balance. *The International Journal of Human Resource Management*, 1755-1776. doi:10.1080/09585192.2015.1075574

Chandarasekar, K. S., Suma, S., Nair, R., & Ansu.S.R. (2013). Study on Work-Life Balance among the executives in IT Industry with special reference to Technopark, Trivandrum, Kerala. *Asian Journal of Multidimensional Research, 2*(3).

Chandaria, I. B. (2013). *Work life balance – A study of dual career couples in medical sector.* Mumbai: Ishita Bharat Chandaria.

Chandra, V. (2012). Work–life balance: eastern and western perspectives. *The International Journal of Human Resource Management, 23*(5), 1040-1056.

Chang, A., McDonald, P., & Burton, P. (2009). *Methodological choices in work-life balance research 1987 to 2006 : a critical review.* Queensland: Taylor & Francis.

Charles, V., & James, E. (2005). Gender, Job Insecurity and the Work-Life Balance. In D. M. Houston, *Work-Life Balance in the 21st Century* (pp. 170-188). New York: Palgrave Macmillan.

Chen, S.-C., Chiang, Y.-H., & Huang, Y.-J. (2015). Exploring the psychological mechanisms linking work-related factors with work–family conflict and work–family facilitation among Taiwanese nurses. *International Journal of Human Resource Management*, 581-602. doi:10.1080/09585192.2015.1118140

Cherry, K. (2017). *The Psychology of Learning* . Retrieved from VerywellMind: https://www.verywellmind.com/learning-study-guide-2795698

Chiorri, C., Bracco, F., Piccinno, T., Modafferi, C., & Battini, V. (2014). Psychometric Properties of a Revised Version of the Ten Item Personality Inventory. *European Journal of Psychological Assesment.*

Chitra Devi, A., & Sheela Rani, S. (2012). Work-Life Balance as a Determinant of Life Satisfaction and Family Satisfaction - A Study among Women in BPO. *International Journal on Information Science and Computing, 6*(1), 15-20.

Choa, E., & Allen, T. D. (2018). The transnational family: A typology and implications for workfamily balance. *Human Resource Management Review.* doi:10.1016/j.hrmr.2018.01.001

Cholasseri, S., & Senthilkumar, R. (2017). Work-Life Balance of College Teachers in Malapuram City. *IJARIIE*, 3843-3854.

Chung, H. (2017). *Work Autonomy, Flexibility and Work-life Balance.* Canterbury: University of Kent.

Cioffi, D. (2018). *College President Perceptions of Personal Wellness: Exploring "Well-ish" and the Work-Life Balance of Mid-Career Private College Presidents.* Ann Arbor: ProQuest.

Clark, S. C. (2000). Work/Family Border Theory: A New Theory of Work/Family Balance. *Human Relations*, 747-770. doi:10.1177/0018726700536001

Clarke, M. C., Koach, L. C., & Hill, E. J. (2004). The Work-Family Interface: Differentiating Balance and Fit. *Family and Consumer Sciences Research Journal, 23*(2), 121-140. doi:10.1177/1077727X04269610

Clifton, A., Turkheimer, E., & Oltmanns, T. F. (2005). Self- and Peer Perspectives on Pathological Personality Traits and Interpersonal Problems. *Psychol Assess*, 121-135.

ConsolaciónAdame-Sánchez, F.González-Cruz, T., & ClaraMartínez-Fuentes. (2016). Do firms implement work–life balance policies to benefit their workers or themselves? *Journal of Business Research, 69*(11), 5519-5523. doi:10.1016/j.jbusres.2016.04.164

Copeland, A. D. (2013). *A Qualitative Study of Clinical Oncology Nurses Perceptions of Work-Life Balance.* Ph.D Thesis, University of Phoenix.

Cornell, J. (2016, September 20). *The Psychoanalytical Theory and the Humanistic Theory. A Critical Comparison*. Retrieved from Linkedin: https://www.linkedin.com/pulse/psychoanalytical-theory-humanistic-critical-josiah-cornell

Corr, P. J., & Matthews, G. (2009). *The Cambridge Handbook of Personality Psychology*. Cambridge: Cambridge University Press.

Corsi, N., Andani, M. E., Tinazzi, M., & Fiorio, M. (2016). Changes in perception of treatment efficacy are associated to the magnitude of the nocebo effect and to personality traits. *Scientific Reports*, 1-11. doi:10.1038/srep30671

Cortland. (2015). *Criticisms and Strengths of Humanistic Psychology*. Retrieved from Cortland: http://web.cortland.edu/andersmd/HUMAN/CRITIC.HTML

Coughlan, D. A. (2005). *WORK-LIFE BALANCE An introduction to work-life balance issues and a preliminary exploration of work-life balance culture in NUI, Maynooth*. Equality Authority. Maynooth : Dr. Ann Coughlan.

Cradden, C. (2014). Institutionalist Pluralism and Public Policy. In C. Cradden, *Neoliberal Industrial Relations Policy in the UK: How the Labour Movement Lost the Argument* (pp. 19-40). London: Palgrave Macmillan.

Crawford, J. E. (2016). *Live Free Or Diy*. Redwood Digital Publishing.

Creswell, J. W. (2013). *Educational Research*. Boston: Pearson.

Creswell, J. W. (2013). *Research Design*. California: Sage.

Creswell, J. W. (2014). *Research design : qualitative, quantitative, and mixed methods approaches*. New Delhi: SAGE Publications, Inc.

Crompton, R., & Lyonette, C. (2006). Work-Life 'Balance' in Europe. *Acta Sociologica*, 379-393. doi:10.1177/0001699306071680

Currie, J. M. (1995). *Welfare and the Well-Being of Children*. (F. Welch, Ed.) Texas: Harwood Academic Publishers.

Dale, A. (2005). Combining Family and Employment: Evidence from Pakistani and Bangladeshi Women. In D. M. Houston, *Work-Life Balance in the 21st Century* (pp. 230-245). New York: Palgrave Macmillan.

Davis, D. W., Finkel, D., Turkheimer, E., & Dickens, W. (2015). Genetic and Environmental Contributions to Behavioral Stability and Change in Children 6-36 Months of Age Using Louisville Twin Study Data. *Behavior Genetics*, 610-621. doi:10.1007/s10519-015-9759-x

Deary, I. J. (2009). The trait approach to personality. In P. J. Corr, & G. Matthews (Eds.), *Cambridge Handbook of Personality Psychology* (pp. 89-109). Cambridge : Cambridge University Press.

Deckman, M. E. (1996). Balancing Work and Family Responsibilities: Flextime and Child Care in the Federal Government. *Public Administration Review, 56*(2), 174-179. doi:10.2307/977205

Dekking, F., Kraaikamp, C., Lopuhaa, H., & Meester, L. (2005). *A Modern Introduction to Probability and Statistics: Understanding Why and How.* Mekelweg: Springer.

Department of Labour New Zealand. (2006). *Work-Life Balance in New Zealand: A snapshot of employee and employer attitudes and experiences.* Wellington: Department of Labour.

Department of Labour Wellington New Zealand. (2004). *Achieving Balanced Livesand Employment; What New Zealanders are Saying about Work-Life Balance.* Wellington: Department of Labour Wellington New Zealand.

Devadoss, A., & Minnie, J. B. (2013). A Study of Personality Influence in Building Work Life Balance Using Fuzzy Relation Mapping (FRM). *International Journal of Data Mining Techniques and Applications*, 211-216.

Dewe, P. J., O'Driscoll, M. P., & Cooper, C. L. (2010). *Coping with Work Stress A Review and Critique.* Malden: John Wiley & Sons Ltd.

Dhanya, J., & Ravi, N. (2017). Work Life Balance of Women Faculty in Professional Colleges of Kerala. *Proceedings of International Conference on Strategies in Volatile and Uncertain Environment for Emerging Markets* (pp. 136-144). New Delhi: Indian Institute of Technology Delhi.

Dhanya.J.S, & D, K. (2016). A Study on Work Life Balance of Teachers in Engineering Colleges in Kerala. *Journal of Chemical and Pharmaceutical Sciences, 9*(4), 2098-2104.

Dhanya.J.S, & Kinslin, D. (2017, January 30). *A study on work life balance of women employees at ULCCS Ltd, Kozhkode*. Retrieved from Resrarchgate.net: https://www.researchgate.net/publication

Dillon, W. R., Kumar, A., & Mulani, N. (1997). Offending Estimates in Covariance Structure Analysis: Comments on the Causes of and Solutions to Heywood Cases . *Psychological Bulletin*, 126-135.

Direnzo, M. S., Greenhaus, J. H., & Weer, C. H. (2016, May). Relationship between Protean Career Orientation and Work-Life Balance: A Resource Perspective. *Journal of Organizational Behavior*, 4-57.

Dissertation Writing. (2016). *Sample Significance of the Study*. Retrieved from Dissertation Writing: https://www.dissertationwriting.biz/dissertation-writing-tips/sample-significance-of-the-study/

Doble, N., & Supriya, M. (2010). Gender Differences in the Perception of Work-Life Balance. *Management*, 331-342.

Dobre, C., & Milovan-Ciuta, A.-M. (2015). Personality Influences Online Stores Consumer Behaviour. *ECOFORUM*, 69-76.

Dollard, M. F., Shimazu, A., Nordin, R. B., Brough, P., & Tuckey, M. R. (2014). The Context of Psychosocial Factors at Work in the Asia Pacific. In M. F. Dollard, A. Shimazu, R. B. Nordin, P. Brough, & M. R. Tuckey, *Psychosocial Factors at Work in the Asia Pacific* (pp. 3-26). Springer.

Dulk, L. d., Groeneveld, S., Ollier-Malaterre, A., & Valcour, M. (2013). National context in work-life research: A multi-level cross-national analysis of the adoption of workplace work-life arrangements in Europe. *uropean Management Journal*, 478-496.

Edgar, F., & Geare, A. (2004). Employee Demographics in Human Resource Management Research. *Research and Practice in Human Resource Management*, 61-91.

Edwards, J. R., & Rothbard, N. P. (2000). Mechanisms linking Work and Family: Clarifying the relationhip between Work and Family Constructs. *Academy of Management Review, 25*(1), 178-199.

Ellis, A. (n.d.). *THE CASE AGAINST RELIGION: A Psychotherapist's View and THE CASE AGAINST RELIGIOSITY* . New York: American Atheist Press.

Employment Market Analysis and Research. (2011). *The Third Work-Life Balance Employee Survey: Technical report.* Victoria Street: Department for Business, Innovation & Skills.

Emslie, C., & Hunt, K. (2009). 'Live to Work' or 'Work to Live'? A Qualitative Study of Gender and Work–life Balance among Men and Women in Mid-life. *Gender, Work and Organization, 16*(2), 151-172.

England, A. D. (2009). *The Essential Guide to Handling Workplace Harassment & Discrimination* (1st ed.). (L. Guerin, Ed.) California, United States OF America: Nolo.

Eraranta, K. (2015). A new Social Risk? Social-Scientific Knowledge and Work-Life Balance in Twentieth-Century Finland. *Social Science History*, 63-83. doi:10.1017/ssh.2015.42

ERIH. (2018). *The Industrial Revolution in Europe.* Retrieved from Europian Route of Industrial Heritage: https://www.erih.net/how-it-started/the-industrial-revolution-in-europe/

Eriksen, C. W. (2008). Chapter 2 Perception and Personality. In R. W. Joseph M. Wepman, *Concepts of Personality* (pp. 31-62). London: Aldine Publishing Company.

Eurofound. (2012). *Working time and work–life balance in a life course perspective.* Dublin: Eurofound.

Eurofound. (2015). *Policies to improve work–life balance .* Retrieved from Eurofound: https://www.eurofound.europa.eu/publications/report/2015/eu-member-states/policies-to-improve-work-life-balance

Eurofound. (2017, October 03). *Working time and work-life balance .* Retrieved from Eurofound: https://www.eurofound.europa.eu/observatories/eurwork/about-eurwork/working-time-and-work-life-balance

Eysenck, H. J. (2012). *A Model for Personality.* New York: Springer Science & Business Media.

Farkiya, R. (2015). *A Study of Work Life Balance in Health Care Industry.* PhD Thesis, Indore.

Fatima, N., & A.Sahibzada, S. (2012). An Empirical Analysis of Factors Affecting Work Life Balance among University Teachers: The case of Pakistan. *Journal of International Academic Research*, 16-28.

Felstead, A., Jewson, N., Phizacklea, A., & Walters, S. (2002). Opportunities to work at home in the context of work-life balance. *Human Resource Management Journal*, 54-76.

Field, A. (2013). *Discovering Statistics Using IBM SPSS Statistics.* New Delhi: SAGE Publications Asia-Pacific Pte Ltd .

Finch, W. H., & F. French, B. (2015). *Latent Variable Modeling R.* New York: Routledge.

Fincham, J. E. (2008). Response Rates and Responsiveness for Surveys, Standards, and the Journal. *American Journal of Pharmaceutical Education*.

Fischer, D. H. (1970). *HISTORIANS' FALLACIES Toward a Logic of Historical Thought.* New Delhi: David Hackett Fischer.

Fisher, G. G., Bulger, C. A., & Smith, C. S. (2009). Beyond Work and Family: A Measure of Work/Nonwork Interference and Enhancement. *Journal of Occupational Health Psychology*, 441-456.

Fisher, K., & Layte, R. (2004). Measuring work-life balance using time diary data. *Electronic International Journal of Time Use Research, 1*(1), 1-13. doi:dx.doi.org/10.13085/eIJTUR.1.1

Fisher-McAuley, G., Stanton, J. M., Jolton, J. A., & Gavin, J. (2003). Modeling the Relationship between Work/Life Balance and Organizational Outcomes. 1-30. Retrieved August 8, 2016, from https://www.researchgate.net/publication/260516221

Fleetwood, S. (2006). *Why work-life balance now?* Lancaster: Lancaster University Management School.

Forrest, S., & Ellis, V. (2006). The making of sexualities: sexuality, identity and equality. In M. Cole, *Education, Equality and Human Rights Oxfordshire Mike Cole Routledge* (pp. 89-110). Oxfordshire : Routledge.

Foucreault, A., Ollier-Malaterre, A., & Ménard, J. (2016). Organizational culture and work–life integration: A barrier to employees' respite? *The*

International Journal of Human Resource Management.
doi:10.1080/09585192.2016.1262890

Foucreault, A., Ollier-Malaterre, A., & Ménard, J. (2017). Organizational culture and work–life integration: A barrier to employees' respite? *The International Journal of Human Resource Management*. doi:10.1080/09585192.2016.1262890

Fra̧tczak, E., & Ptak-Chmielewska, A. (2013). The Interplay of Fertility Intentions, Female Employment and Work–Life Balance Policies in Contemporary Poland: Can Gender Equity, Preference and Social Capital Theories Provide a Better Insight? In L. S. Oláh, & E. Fra̧tczak, *Childbearing, Women's Employment and Work–Life Balance Policies in Contemporary Europe* (pp. 135-178). New York: Palgrave Macmillan.

Fradelos, E., Kourakos, M., Zyga, S., & Papathanasiou, I. V. (2017). Measuring Religiosity in Nursing: Reliability, Validity and Psychometric Properties of the Greek Translation of The Centrality of Religiosity Scale -15. *American Journal of Nursing Science*, 25-32. doi:10.11648/j.ajns.s.2018070301.14

Francis, V., Fulu, E., & Lingard, H. (2009). Is it a problem? In H. Lingard, & V. Francis, *Managing Work–Life Balance in Construction* (pp. 1-38). Oxon: Spon Press.

Frone, M. R. (2003). Work-family balance. In *Handbook of occupational health psychology* (pp. 143-162). Washington: American Psychological Association.

Frone, M. R., Rusell, M., & Cooper, M. L. (1994). Relationship between Job and Family Satisfaction: Casual or Noncasual Covariation? *Journal of Management, 20*(3), 565-579.

Frone, M. R., Russell, M., & Cooper, M. L. (1992). Antecedents and Outcomes of Work-Family Conflict: Testing a Model of the Work-Family Interface. *Journal of Applied Psychology, 77*(1), 65-78. doi:10.1037//0021-9010.77.1.65

Frone, M. R., Russell, M., & Cooper, M. L. (1992). Prevalence of workfamily conflict: Are work and family boundaries asymmetrically permeable? *Journal of Organizational Behavior*, 723-729.

Frone, M. R., Yardley, J. K., & Markel, K. S. (1997). Developing and Testing an Integrative Model of the Work–Family Interface. *Journal of Vocational Behavior*, 145-167.

Furnham, A. (2013). *The Resilient Manager.* New York: Palgrave Macmillan. doi:10.1057/9781137361073

Gambles, R., Lewis, S., & Rapoport, R. (2006). *The Myth of Work–Life Balance.* West Sussex : John Wiley & Sons Ltd.

Ganiyu, I., Fields, Z., & Atiku, S. (2017). Work-life balance strategies, work-family satisfaction and employees' job performance in Lagos, Nigeria's manufacturing sector. *Journal of Contemporary Management*, 441-460.

Gaskin, J. (2011). Multigroup Moderation in AMOS (chi-square difference).

Gatrell, C. J., & Cooper, C. L. (2008). Work-life balance: working for whom? *European Journal of International Management, 2*(6), 71-86. Retrieved from www.inderscience.com/ejim

Gaus, G. F. (2003). *Contemporary Theories of Liberalism.* (I. Hollida, Ed.) London: Sage Publication.

Gehrke, A., & Hassard, J. (2015, January 26). *Work-life balance – Managing the interface between family and working life.* Retrieved from OSH WIKI: https://oshwiki.eu/wiki/Work-life_balance_Managing_the_interface_between_family_and_working_life

Geld, P. V., Oosterveld, P., Heck, G. V., & Kuijpers-Jagtman, A. M. (2007). Smile Attractiveness. *The Angle Orthodontist*, 759-765.

Gendera, S. (2011). Gaining an insight into Central European transnational care spaces: Migrant live-in care workers in Austria. In M. Bommes, & G. Sciortino, *Foggy Social Structures Irregular Migration, European Labour Markets and the Welfare State* (pp. 91-116). Amsterdam: Amsterdam University Press.

Geron, S., & Atalia, W. (2005). Influence of Sex on the Perception of Oral and Smile Esthetics with Different Gingival Display and Incisal Plane Inclination. *The Angle Orthodontist*, 778-784.

Ghanbaria, A., Ramazanib, M., & Jaliliniac, M. (2013). Analysis of work-life balance from the viewpoint of Iranian accountants. *Management Science Letters* , 2315-2322.

Gora, S. (2015). *Know Your Self for Better Work-Life Balance.* Mumbai: BecomeShakespeare.com.

Gosling, S. D., Rentfrow, P. J., & Swann, W. B. (2003). A very brief measure of Big-Five personality domain. *Journal of Research in Personality*, 204-528. doi:10.1016/S0092-6566(03)00046-1

Govrenment of India, Central Statistics Office. (2017). *Selected Socio-Economic Statistics India 2017.* New Delhi: Central Statistics Office Social Statistics Division.

Gowgisk, N. S. (2015). *Stress and Work/Life Balance among Employees of Manufacturing and IT Sector.* PhD Thesis, Universityof Mysore, Department of Studies in Social Work, Mysore.

Goz Lab. (2013). *Ten Item Personality Measure (TIPI).* Retrieved from Goz Lab.

Graham, G. (2007). *Behaviorism.* Retrieved from Stanford Encyclopedia of Philosophy.

Graziano, W. G., & Tobin, R. M. (2013). Agreeableness. In M. R. Leary, & R. H. Hoyle, *Handbook of Individual Differences in Social Behavior* (pp. 46-61). New York: Guilford Publications.

Green, J. (2012). The Agricultural Revolution: Crash Course World History 1. Indianapolis, Indiana, United States. Retrieved January 15, 2015

Greenberg, C. L., & Avigdor, B. S. (2009). *What Happy Working Mothers Know.* New Jersey: John Wiley & Sons, Inc.

Greenhaus, J. H., & Allen, T. D. (2002). Work-Family Balance a Review and Extension of Literature. In J. C. Quick, & L. E. Tetrick, *Hand Book of Occupational Health and Psychology* (pp. 165-183). Washington: American Psychological Association.

Greenhaus, J. H., & Beutell, N. J. (1985). Sources of Conflict between Work and Family Roles. *The Academy of Management Review, 10*(1), 76-88. Retrieved April 8, 2016, from http://www.jstor.org/stable/258214

Greenhaus, J. H., & Brummelhuis, L. L. (2013). Models and frameworks underlying work–life research. In *Handbook of work–life integration among professionals* (p. 1434).

Greenhaus, J. H., & Powell, G. N. (2006). When the Work and Family are Allies: A Theory of Work-Family Enrichment. *Academy of Management Review, 31*(1), 72-92.

Greenhaus, J. H., Collins, K. M., & Shaw, J. D. (2003). The relation between work-life balance and quality of life. *Journal of Vocational Behavior*, 510-531. doi:10.1016/S0001-8791(02)00042-8

Gregory, A., & Milner, S. (2011). Fathers and work-life balance in France and the UK : policy and practice. 1-20. doi:10.1108/01443331111104797

Greubel, J., Arlinghaus, A., Nachreiner, F., & Lombardi, D. A. (2016). Higher risks when working unusual times? A cross-validation of the effects on safety, health, and work–life balance. *International Archives of Occupational and Environmental Health*. doi:10.1007/s00420-016-1157-z

Gröpel, P., & Kuhl, J. (2011). Work–life balance and subjective well-being: The mediating role of need fulfilment. *British Journal of Psychology*, 365-375. doi:10.1348/000712608X337797

Grzywacz, J. G. (2000). Work-Family Spillover and Health During Midlife: Is Managing Conflict Everything? *The Science of Health Promotion*, 236-243.

Grzywacz, J. G., & Bass, B. L. (2003). Work, family, and mental health: Testing different models of work-family fit. *Journal of Marriage and Family*, 248-261.

Grzywacz, J. G., & Marks, N. F. (2000). Family, Work, Work-Family Spillover, and Problem Drinking During Midlife. *Journal of Occupational Health Psychology*, 111-126.

Grzywacz, J., & S.Carlson, D. (2007, November). Conceptualizing Work–Family Balance: Implications for Practice and Research. *Advances in Developing Human Resources, 9*(4), 455-471. doi:10.1177/1523422307305487

Guest, D. E. (2002). Perspectives on the Study of Work-life Balance. *Social Science Information, 42*(2), 255-279. doi:10.1177/0539018402041002005

Gurney, S. (2009). *Gender, work-life balance and health amongst women and men in administrative, manual and technical jobs in a single organisation: a qualitative study.* University of Glasgow . Glasgow : University of Glasgow. Retrieved from http://theses.gla.ac.uk/1641/

Haar, J. M., & Bardoel, A. (2007). Work Family Positive Spillover Predicting Outcomes: A study of Australian Employees. Victoria: Australian Centre for Research in Employment and Work.

Haar, J. M., Roche, M., & Brummelhuis, L. t. (2017). A daily diary study of work-life balance in managers: utilizing a daily process model. *The International Journal of Human Resource Management.* doi:10.1080/09585192.2017.1314311

Haar, J. M., Roche, M., & Taylor, D. (2012). Work-family conflict and turnover intentions amongst indigenous employees: The importance of the whanau/family for Maori. *The International Journal of Human Resource Management*, 2546-2560. doi:10.1080/09585192.2011.610344

Haddon, B., Hede, A., & Whiteoak, J. (2009). Work-Life Balance: Towards an Integrated Conceptual Framework.

Hakim, C. (2005). Sex Differences in Work-Lift, Balance Goals. In D. M. Houston, *Work-Life Balance in the 21st Century* (pp. 55-79). New York: Palgrave Macmillan.

Hall, A. (2018). *Which Employment Benefit does your Staff Value Most.* Retrieved from The Olson Group: https://theolsongroup.com/company-benefits-employees-value/

Hall, D. T., & Richter, J. (1989). Balancing Work Life and Home Life: What Can Organizations Do to Help? *The Academy of Management Executive*, 213-223. Retrieved from http://www.jstor.org/stable/4164832

Hammer, L. B., Cullen, J. C., B, N. M., Sinclair, R. R., & Shafiro, M. V. (2005). The longitudinal effects of work-family conflict and positive spillover on depressive symptoms among dual-earner couples. *Journal of Occupational Health Psychology, 10*(2), 138-154.

Hämmig, O., & Bauer, G. (2009). Work-life imbalance and mental health among male and female employees in Switzerland. *International Journal of Public Health*, 88-95. doi:10.1007/s00038-009-8031-7

Happell, B. (2008). The importance of clinical experience for mental health nursing - part 2: relationships between undergraduate nursing students' attitudes, preparedness, and satisfaction. *International Journal of Mental Health Nursing*, 333-340.

Haslam, D., Filus, A., Morawska, A., Sanders, M. R., & Fletcher, R. (2014, June). The Work–Family Conflict Scale (WAFCS): Development and Initial Validation of a Self-report Measure of Work–Family Conflict for Use with Parents. *Child Psychiatry and Human Development*. doi:10.1007/s10578-014-0476-0

Haslam, N. (2007). 1 What is Personality? In N. Haslam, C. McGarty, & S. A. Haslam (Eds.), *Introduction to Personality and Intelligence* (pp. 3-12). London: Sage Publications Ltd.

Hayman, J. (2005). Psychometric Assessment of an Instrument Designed to Measure Work Life Balance. *Research and Practice in Human Resource Management, 13*(1), 85-91.

Heap, D. (2005). Characteristics of People Employed in the Public Sector. In O. o. Statistics, *National Statistics Features* (pp. 489-500). Drummond Gate: Office of National Statistics, U.K.

Heck, R. H., Thomas, S. L., & Tabata, L. N. (2010). *Multilevel and Longitudional Modeling with IBM SPSS.* London: Routledge.

Heck, R. H., Thomas, S. L., & Tabata, L. N. (2011). *Multilevel and Longitudinal Modeling with IBM SPSS.* 270 Madison Avenue New York, NY 10016: Routledge Taylor & Francis Group.

Hildenbrand, K. (2016). *Helping in Finding the Right Balance: Leadership, Work-Family Balance, and Employee Outcomes.* Aston: Kristin Hildenbrand.

Hill, E. J., Hawkins, A. J., Ferris, M., & Weitzman, M. (2001). Finding an Extra Day a Week: The Positive Influence of Perceived Job Flexibility on Work and Family Life Balance. *Family Relations*, 49-58.

Hill, E. J., Miller, B. C., Weiner, S. P., & Colihan, J. (1998). Influences of the virtual office on aspects of work and work/life balance. *Personnel Psychology, 51*(3), 667-683.

Hilla, E. J., Grzywaczb, J. G., Allena, S., Blancharda, V. L., Matz-Costac, C., Shulkinc, S., & Pitt-Catsouphesc, M. (2008). Defining and conceptualizing workplace flexibility. *Community, Work & Family*, 149-163. doi:10.1080/13668800802024678

Hindustan Times. (2016). *Sikkim the best place to work for women, Delhi at bottom of list: Report.* Hindustan Times.

Hirschi, A., Shockley, K. M., & Zacher, H. (in press). Achieving work-family balance: An action regulation model. *Academy of Management Review.*

History. (2017). *Industrial Revolution.* Retrieved from History.com: https://www.history.com/topics/industrial-revolution

Hobson, C. J., Delunas, L., & Kesic, D. (2001). Compelling evidence of the need for corporate work/life balance initiatives: results from a national survey of stressful life-events. *Journal of Employment Counseling*, 8-44.

Hofmans, J., Kuppens, P., & Allik, J. (2008). Is short in length short in content? An examination of the domain representation Personality and Individual Differences. *Personality and Individual Differences.*

Holahan, C. K., & Gilbert, L. A. (1979). Interrole conflict for working women: Careers versus jobs. *ournal of Applied Psychology*, 86-90. doi:10.1037/0021-9010.64.1.86

Hollinger, F., & Eder, A. (2016). Functional Equivalence and validity of rligiousness indicators in cross-cultural comparative surveys . *Methodological Innovations*, 1-12. doi:10.1177/2059799115622756

Holter, Ø. G. (2007). Men's Work and Family Reconciliation in Europe. *Men and Masculinities*, 425-456.

Houston, D. M. (2005). Work-Life Balance in the 21st Century . In D. M. Houston, *Work-Life Balance in the 21st Century* (pp. 1-10). Palgrave Macmillan.

Hoyle, R. H. (Ed.). (2012). *Handbook of Structural equation modeling.* Spring Street, New York, NY 10012 : The Guilford Press.

Huber, S., & Huber, O. W. (2012). The Centrality of Religiosity Scale (CRS). *Religions, 3*, 710-724. doi:10.3390/rel3030710

Hubert, S. (2014). *The Impact of Religiosity on Fertility A Comparative Analysis of France, Hungary, Norway, and Germany.* Bochum: Springer.

Hutcheson, P. G. (2012). *Work-Life Balance.* Georgia: IEEE-USA.

IBRD. (2017). *Service Sector Employment.* World Bank.

ILO. (2018, April 4). *International Labour Standards on Work-Life Balance.* Retrieved from ILO: http://www.ilo.org/travail/areasofwork/WCMS_249047/lang--en/index.htm

Ingham, G. (2007). *Motivate People Getting the Best from Yourself and Others.* London: Dorling Kindersley Limited .

International Labour Organisation. (2011 , November 19). Work–life balance. *Policy Development Section Employment and Social Protection Segment.* Geneva: International Labour Organisation.

International Labour Organisation. (2011). *Work–life balance.* Geneva: ILO.

Isdell, L. (2016). *Work-Family Balance among Mothers who are Mid-Career Student Affairs Administrators at Institutions Recognized for Work-Life Policies.* Master Degree Thesis, University of Kansas.

Israel, J. (2010). *A Revolution of the Mind.* Woodstock: Princeton University Press.

Jacquette, D. (2014). *Ontology.* London: Routledge.

Jain, M. (2017). *4 Main Stages of Industrial Revolution.* Retrieved from Your Article Library: http://www.yourarticlelibrary.com/industrial-engineering-2/4-main-stages-of-industrial-revolution/90115

Jayakar, T. J., & Babu, S. S. (2012). Professional Communication for Better Work-Life Balance. *Journal of Education and Practice, 3*(6), 37-46. Retrieved from www.iiste.org

Jeronimus, B. F. (2015). Chapter 1 Introduction . In B. F. Jeronimus, *Environmental Influences on Neuroticism A story about emotional (in)stability* (pp. 7-32). Netherlands: Ridderprint.

Jeswani, S., & Dave, S. (2012). Impact of Individual Personality on Turnover Intention A Study on Faculty Members. *Management and Labour Studies,* 253-265.

Jindal, M. (2016). A Study on Work-life Balance of Working Women in Service Sector. *International Journal of Research in Finance and Marketing*, 14-21.

John, O. P., & Srivastava, S. (1999). The Big-Five Trait Taxonomy: History, Measurement, and Theoretical Perspectives. In *Handbook of personality: Theory and research (2nd ed.).* New York: Guilford.

Jones, K. (2018). *Work-Life Balance: Organizational Leadership and Individual Strategies among Successful Women Real Estate Brokers.* Ph.D, Pepperdine University , Graduate School of Education and Psychology.

Joseph, J., & Sebastian, D. J. (2017). Work-life Balance a Conceptual Review. *Mirror.*

Joseph, J., & Sebastian, D. J. (2017). Work-life balance vs Work-Family Balance - An Evaluation of Scope. *Amity Global HRM Review*, 54-65.

Joshin Joseph, D. J. (2017). Do the Demographics have the potential to influence Work-Life Conflict? *International Journal of Research Culture Society*, 166-171.

Journal Psyche. (2017). *Processing Information with Nonconscious Mind*. Retrieved from Journal Psyche: http://journalpsyche.org/tag/freudian-paradigm/

Kacmar, K. M., Crawford, W. S., Carlson, D. S., Ferguson, M., & Whitten, D. (2014). A Short and Valid Measure of Work-Family Enrichment. *Journal of Occupational Health Psychology, 19*(1), 32-45. doi:10.1037/a0035123

Kakkar, J., & Bhandari, A. (2016). A Study on Work-Life Balance in the Indian Service Sector from a Gender Perspective. *IUP Journal of Organizational Behavior*, 35-56.

Kalliath, P., Kalliath, T., Chan, X. W., & Chan, C. (2018). Linking Work–Family Enrichment to Job Satisfaction through Job Well-Being and Family Support: A Moderated Mediation 5Analysis of Social Workers across India. *British Journal of Social Work*, 1-22.

Kalliath, T., & Brough, P. (2008). Work–life balance: A review of the meaning of the balance construct. *Journal of Management & Organization , 14*(3), 323-327.

Kaur, J. (2013). WORK-LIFE BALANCE: ITS CORRELATION WITH SATISFACTION WITH LIFE AND PERSONALITY DIMENSIONS AMONGST COLLEGE TEACHERS. *International Journal of Marketing, Financial Services & Management Research, 8*(2), 24-35. Retrieved from www.indianresearchjournals.com

Kaur, S., & Misra, K. C. (2013). Nexus between Work Life Balance Practices and Employee Retention – The Mediating Effect of a Supportive Culture. *Asian Social Science, 9*(11), 63-69. doi:10.5539/ass.v9n11p63

Kawamoto, T., & Endo, T. (2015). Genetic and Environmental Contributions to Personality Trait Stability and Change Across Adolescence: Results From a Japanese Twin Sample. *Twin Research and Human Genetics, 18*(5), 545-556. doi:10.1017/thg.2015.47

Keeton, K., Fenner, D. E., Johnson, T. R., & Hayward, R. A. (2007). Predictors of Physician Career Satisfaction, Work–Life Balance, and Burnout. *Obetetrics & Gynecology*, 949-955.

Keith, T. Z. (2015). *Multipl Regression and Beyond.* New York: Taylor & Francis.

Kelley, D. (2014). *The Art of Reasoning An Introduction to Logic and Critical Thinking.* London: W. W. Norton & Company .

Kelly, J. (2006). Women thirty-five years on: still unequal after all this time. In M. Cole, *Education, Equality and Human Rights* (pp. 7-21). Oxfordshire : Routledge.

Kelly, M. (2011). *Off Balance Getting Beyond the Work-Life Balance Myth to Personal and Professional Satisfaction.* New York: Hudson Street Press.

Kendler, H. H. (2005). Psychology and Phenomenology: A Clarification. *American Psychologist*, 318-324. doi:10.1037/0003-066X.60.4.318

Killam, L. (2013). *Research terminology simplified: Paradigms, axiology, ontology, epistemology and methodology.* Sudbury, ON: Laura Killam.

Kirchmeyer, C. (1992). Perceptions of Nonwork-to-Work Spillover: Challenging the Common View of Conflict-Ridden Domain Relationships. *Basic and Applied Social Psychology*, 231-249. doi:10.1207/s15324834basp1302_7

Kirchmeyer, C. (1992). Nonwork Participation and Work Attitudes: A Test of Scarcity vs. Expansion Models of Personal Resources. *Human Relations*, 775-795. doi:10.1177/001872679204500802

Kirchmeyer, C. (1995). Managing the Work-Nonwork Boundary: An Assessment of Organizational Responses. *Human Relations*, 515-536. doi:10.1177/001872679504800504

Kirchmeyer, C. (2000). Work-life initiatives: Greed or benevolence regarding workers' time? In *Trends in organizational behavior* (pp. 79-93). New York: John Wiley & Sons Ltd.

Kiuchi, A. (2006). Independent and interdependent self-construals: Ramifications for a multicultural society. *Japanese Psychological Research*, 1-16. doi:10.1111/j.1468-5884.2006.00300.x

Kodz, J., Harper, H., & Dench, S. (2002). *Work-Life Balance: Beyond the Rhetoric.* Brighton: The Institute for Employment Studies. Retrieved from http://www.employment-studies.co.uk

Kofodimos, J. R. (1993). Balancing act: How managers can integrate successful careers and fulfilling personal lives. *The Jossey-Bass management series*.

Kong, M. Y. (2015). Balance is in the Moment. *Frontiers in Pediatrics*, 1-3. doi:10.3389/fped.2015.00087

Kopelman, R. E., Greenhaus, J., & Connolly, T. F. (1983). A model of work, family, and interrole conflict: A construct validation study. *Organizational Behavior & Human Performance*, 198-215.

Kossek, E. E., & Lee, K.-H. (2017). Work-Family Conflict and Work-Life Conflict . *Oxford Research Encyclopedia of Business and Management*, 23-33.

Kramer, M. H. (2018, May). *What Employees Value Most* . Retrieved from The Balance Careers: https://www.thebalancecareers.com/what-employees-value-most-125667

Krings, B.-J., Nierling, L., Pedaci, M., & Piersanti, M. (2009). *Working time, gender and work-life balance.* Luxembourg: Europian Commission.

Kumar, C. (2018). *India lost 11.73 lakh man days to strikes in 2017.* Kochi: Times of India.

Kumari, S. V. (2017). *An Emprical Study on Work Life Balance of an Employee With Special Reference to Telecom Sector.* ST Peter's University Chennai. Chennai: Un-Published Thesis.

Kumari, S., & Selvi, A. (2015). An Exploratory Study Of Work Life Balance Emanates And Work Satisfaction In Ericsson Company-Chennai City. *International Journal of scientific research and management*, 3565-3570.

Kundnani, N., & Mehta, P. (2014). Role of Personality Traits in Work-Life Balance. *International Journal of Management Research & Review*, 722-731.

Kurowska, A. (2018). Gendered Effects of Home-Based Work on Parents' Capability to Balance Work with Non-work: Two Countries with Different Models of Division of Labour Compared. *Social Indicators Research*. doi:10.1007/s11205-018-2034-9

Lakshmi, K. S., Ramachandran, T., & Boohene, D. (2012). Analysis of Work Life Balance of Female Nurses in Hospitals - Comparative Study between Government and Private Hospital in Chennai, TN., India. *International Journal of Trade, Economics and Finance*, 213-218.

Lakshmipriya, & Krishna, R. (2016). Work Life Balance and Implications Of Spill Over Theory – A Study on Women Entrepreneurs. *International Journal of Research in IT & Management*, 96-109.

Lavassani, K. M., & Movahedi, B. (2014). Developments in Theories And Measures of Work-Family Relationships: From Conflict to Balance. *Contemporary Research on Organization Management and Administration, 2*(1), 6-18.

Lawell, L. (2012). *42 Rules for Working Moms.* California: Super Star Press.

Lazar, I., Osoian, C., & Ratiu, P. (2010). The Role of Work-Life Balance Practices in Order to Improve Organizational Performance. *European Research Studies*, 201-214.

Leaptrott, J., & McDonald, J. M. (2011). The conflict between work and family roles: the effects on managers' reliance on information sources in dealing with significant workplace events. *Journal of Organizational Culture, Communications and Conflict*, 132-148.

Lenhard, W., & Lenhard, A. (2016). *Calculation of Effect Sizes.* Retrieved from Psychometrica: https://www.psychometrica.de/effect_size.html

Lewis, S. (1997). 'Family Friendly' Employment Policies: A Route to Changing Organizational Culture or Playing About at the Margins? *Gender Work and Organization*, 13-23. doi:10.1111/1468-0432.00020

Lewis, S., & Beauregard, T. A. (2018). The Meanings of Work-Life Balance: A cultural perspective . In *The Cambridge handbook of the global work-family interface* (pp. 720-732). Cambridge: Cambridge University Press.

Lewis, S., & Lewis, J. (1997). Work, family and well-being. Can the law help? (P. Taylor, Ed.) *Legal and Criminological Psychology, 2*(2), 155-167. doi:10.1111/j.2044-8333.1997.tb00340.x

Lewis, S., Gambles, R., & Rapoport, R. (2007). The constraints of a 'work–life balance' approach: an international perspective. *International Journal of Human Resource*, 360-373.

Leyden, M. (2012). *There's No Place like Home: Perceived Powerlessness and Work-Life Balance of Male Residential Construction Workers in Southern Ontario.* University of Guelph, Department of Sociology. Guelph, Ontario: University of Guelph.

Li, M., & Jie-lin, Y. (2012). An Empirical Study on the Effect of Work/Life Commitment to Work-Life Conflict. *2012 International Conference on Applied Physics and Industrial Engineering* (pp. 1343-1349). Elsevier.

Li, Y. (2018). Effects of Work-Life Balance on Organizational Commitment: A Study in China's State-Owned Enterprise. *World Journal of Social Science Research*, 144-166. doi:10.22158/wjssr.v5n2p144

Lilly, J. D. (2006). The effect of personality on perceptions of justice. *Journal of Managerial Psychology*, 438-458.

Lingard, H., Francis, V., & Turner, M. (2009). Social policy and legal frameworks. In H. Lingard, & V. Francis, *Managing Work–Life Balance in Construction* (pp. 38-76). Oxon: Spon Press.

Literature reviews. (2016). Retrieved from Royal Literary Fund: https://www.rlf.org.uk/

Littig, B. (2008). Work Life Balance – catchword or catalyst for sustainable work? *Reihe Soziologie / Sociological Series 85* , 1-14. Retrieved from http://www.ihs.ac.at

Lockwood, N. R. (2003). Work/Life Balance: Challenges and Solutions. *SHRM Research Quarterly*.

Lowe, E. J. (2013). *Forms of Thought A Study in Philosophical Logic.* New York: Cambridge University Press.

Lucia-Casademunt, A. M., García-Cabrera, A. M., & Cuéllar-Molina, D. G. (2015). National culture, work-life balance and employee well-being in European tourism firms: the moderating effect of uncertainty avoidance values. *Tourism & Management Studies*, 62-69.

Lumen. (2017). *Psychodynamic Perspectives on Personality*. Retrieved from Lumen Boundless Personality: https://courses.lumenlearning.com/boundless-psychology/chapter/psychodynamic-perspectives-on-personality

Lumen Boundless Personality. (2017). *Trait Perspectives on Personality*. Retrieved from Lumen Boundless Personality: https://courses.lumenlearning.com/boundless-psychology/chapter/trait-perspectives-on-personality/

Lutz, K., Boehnke, M., Huinink, J., & Tophoven, S. (2013). Female Employment, Reconciliation Policies and Childbearing Intentions in East and West Germany . In L. S. Oláh, & E. Fratczak, *Childbearing, Women's Employment and Work–Life Balance Policies in Contemporary Europe* (pp. 97-134). New York: Palgrave Macmillan.

Lyness, K. S., & Judiesch, M. K. (2014). Gender Egalitarianism and Work–Life Balance for Managers: Multisource Perspectives in 36 Countries. *Appilied Psychology: An International Review*, 96-129. doi:10.1111/apps.12011

M.Muck, P., Hell, B., & Gosling, S. D. (2007). Construct Validation of a Short Five-Factor Model Instrument . *European Journal of Psychological Assessment* , 166-175.

Machin, M. A., & Sankey, K. S. (2008). Relationships between young drivers'personality characteristics, risk perceptions, and driving behaviour . *Accident Analysis and Perception*, 1-13.

Major, V. S., Klein, K. J., & Ehrhart, M. G. (2002). Work Time, Work Interference With Family, and Psychological Distress. *Journal of Applied Psychology, 87*(3), 427-436. doi:10.1037//0021-9010.87.3.427

Malik, M. I., Zaheer, A., Khan, M. A., & Ahmed, M. (2010). Developing and Testing a Model of Burnout at Work and Turnover Intensions among Doctors in Pakistan. *International Journal of Business and Management, 5*(10), 234-247. Retrieved from www.ccsenet.org/ijbm

Mann, R. D. (1959). A review of Relationship Between Personality and Performance in Small Groups. *Psychological Bulletin*, 241-270.

Marks, S., & MacDermid, S. M. (1996). Multiple Roles and the Self: A Theory of Role Balance. *Journal of Marriage and the Family, 58*(2), 417-432.

Martin, J. (2006). Gender and education: change and continuity. In M. Cole, *Education, Equality and Human Rights* (pp. 22-42). Oxfordshire : Routledge.

Martin, L. K. (2016). *Norway Leads the World in Gender Equality and Work-Life Balance: A Qualitative Life Course Study of Norwegian Women.* Ph.D Thesis.

Mathew, R. V., & Panchanatham, N. (2011). An Exploratory study on the Work-Life Balance of Women Entrepreneures in South India. *Asian Academy of Management Journal*, 77-105.

Matsushita, S. (2016). *Ledger Nano S: Bitcoin and Ethereum Hardware Wallet Beginners Guide .*

Matsushita, S. (2017). *New Assets - Ride on the Cryptocurrency Wave!: Step by Step Guide to build The Fastest Growing Assets.* Kindle Edition.

Matthews, G., Deary, I. J., & Whiteman, M. C. (2003). *Personality Traits.* Cambridge: Cambridge University Press.

Maxwell, G. (2008). *Case Study Series on Work-Life Balance in Large Organizations.* Alexandria: Society for Human Resource Management.

Mazerolle, S. M., & Goodman, A. (2013). Fulfillment of Work–Life Balance From the Organizational Perspective: A Case Study. *Journal of Athletic Training, 48*, 668-667. doi:10.4085/1062-6050-48.3.24

McCare, R. R., & Paul T. Costa, J. (1999). A Five Factor Theory of Personality. In *Handbook of Personality: Theory and Research* (pp. 139-153). New York.

McCarthy, A., Darcy, C., & Grady, G. (2010). Work-life balance policy and practice: Understanding line manager attitudes and behaviors. *Human Resource Management Review*, 158-167. doi:10.1016/j.hrmr.2009.12.001

McCrae, R. R. (2009). The Five-Factor Model of personality traits: consensus and controversy. In P. J. Corr, & G. Matthews (Eds.), *The Cambridge Handbook of Personality Psychology* (pp. 148-161). Cambridge: Cambridge University Press.

McCrae, R. R., & Costa, P. T. (2003). Personality in adulthood: A Five-Factor Theory perspective. New York: Guilford Press.

McCrae, R. R., & Sutin, A. R. (2009). Openness to Experience. In M. R. Leary, & R. H. Hoyle, *Handbook of Individual Differences in Social Behavior* (pp. 257-273). New York: Guilford Publications.

McGregor, L., Eveleigh, M., Syler, J. C., & Davis, S. F. (1991). Self-perception of personality characteristics and the Type A behavior pattern. *Bulletin of the Psychonomic Society*, 320-322.

McLeod, S. (2015). *Humanism*. Retrieved from Simply Psychology: https://www.simplypsychology.org/humanistic.html

McLeod, S. (2017). *Behaviorist Approach*. Retrieved from Simply Psychology: https://www.simplypsychology.org/behaviorism.html

McLeod, S. (2017). *Psychodynamic Approach*. Retrieved from Simply Psychology: https://www.simplypsychology.org/psychodynamic.html

McMillan, H. S., Morris, M. L., & Atchley, E. K. (2008). Constructs of the Work/Life Interface and their Importance to HRD. *Academy of Human Resource Development International Research Conference in the Americas.* Panama: ERIC.

McNamaraa, T. K., Pitt-Catsouphesa, M., Matz-Costaa, C., Brownb, M., & Valcourc, M. (2013). Across the continuum of satisfaction with work–family balance: Work hours, flexibility-fit, and work–family culture. *Social Science Research*, 283-298.

Medium. (2017, October 10). *How to create long-term CryptoCurrency portfolio (My top long-term picks)*. Retrieved from Medium: https://medium.com/@EthereumRussian/how-to-create-long-term-cryptocurrency-portfolio-my-top-long-term-picks-b415b8320747

Meenakshi, A., & Bhuvaneshwari, M. (2013). Work Organisation and Work-Life Balance in the BPO Sector. *International Journal of Scientific and Research Publications, 3*(6), 1-4.

Meenakshi, S. P., Subrahmanyam, C. V., & Ravichandran, K. (2013). The Importance of Work-Life-Balance. *IOSR Journal of Business and Management*, 31-35.

Merkle, E. C., & You, D. (2018). *Getting Started with nonnest2 .*

Mertens, D. M. (2010). *Research and Education in Educational Psychology.* New Delhi: Sage.

Milkie, M. A., & Peltola, P. (1999). Playing All the Roles: Gender and the Work-Family Balancing Act. *Journal of Marriage and the Family, 61*(2), 476-490. Retrieved from http://www.jstor.org/stable/353763

Mischel, W. (2009). From Personality and Assesment to (1968), Persoanlity Science, 2009. *Journal of Research in Personality*, 282-290. doi:10.1016/j.jrp.2008.12.037

Mitchell, M. L., & Jolley, J. M. (2010). *Research Design Explained.* Wadsworth, Cengage Learning: Macmillan.

Mohanty, A., & Jena, L. K. (2016). Work-Life Balance Challenges for Indian Employees: Socio-Cultural Implications and Strategies. *Journal of Human Resource and Sustainability Studies*, 15-21.

Money, J. B., & Peter, A. J. (2014). Impact of Emotional Intelligence on Work Life Balance – A Global Perspective. *Journal of Exclusive Management Science, 3*(3), 1-8.

Monica.M. (2015, June). A study on work life balance at State Bank of Mysore. *International Journal of in Multidisciplinary and Academic Research (SSIJMAR), 4*(3), 1-15. Retrieved from www.ssijmar.in

Morganson, V. J., Litano, M. L., & O'Neill, S. K. (2014). Promoting Work–Family Balance Through Positive Psychology: A Practical Review of the

Literature. *The Psychologist-Manager Journal, 17*(4), 221-244. doi:10.1037/mgr0000023

Moshoeu, A. N. (2017). *A Model of Personality Traits and Work-Life Balance As Determinants of Employee Engangement.* University of South Africa. Abigail Ngokwana Moshoeu.

Mostert, K., & Oldfield, G. (2011). Work-home interaction of employees in the mining industry. *South African Journal of Economic and Management Sciences.*

Mugeanyi, N. (2017, July). *Work Life Balance: The Need for Self Awareness and Care.* Retrieved from Researchgate.net: https://www.researchgate.net/publication/318910632

Mukhtar, F. (2012). *Work life balance and job satisfaction among faculty at Iowa State University.* Iowa State University . Iowa: Farah Mukhtar.

Murray, A. H. (2008). Chapter 1 Introduction. In H. A. Murray, *Explorations in Personality* (pp. 3-35). New York: Oxford University Press.

Muthukumar, M., Savitha, R., & Kannadas, P. (2014). Work LIFE Balance. *Global Journal of Finance and Management, 6*(9), 827-832.

Nabong, T., & Trønnes, H. (2016). *A Delicate Balance? A study of work-life conflicts, work-life enrichment, and worklife balance among management consultants in Norway.* Bergen: Norwegian School of Economics Bergen.

Naik, P. (1998). *Behaviorism as a Theory of Personality: A Critical Look.* Retrieved from The SAPA Project: http://www.personalityresearch.org/papers/naik.html

Naithani, P. (2010). Overview of Work-Life Balance Discourse and Its Relevance in Current Economic Scenario. *Asian Social Science*, 148-155. Retrieved from www.ccsenet.org/ass

Nelson, P., & McNaughton, T. (2004). New Zealands' Progress on Work-Life Balance: A Work in Progress. *Labour, Employment and Work in New Zealand*, 2017-220.

Netemeyer, R. G., Boles, J. S., & McMurrian, R. (1996). Development and Validation of Work-Family Conflict and Family-Work Conflict Scales. *Journal of Applied Psychology, 81*(4), 400-410.

Neyer, F. J., & Lehnart, J. (2006). Personality, Relationships, and Health: A Dynamic-transactional Perspective. In M. E. Vollrath, *Handbook of Personality and Health* (pp. 95-214). The Atrium, Southern Gate, Chichester, West Sussex : John Wiley & Sons Ltd.

Nomaguchi, K., & Milkie, M. A. (2011). *Gender, Beliefs about Spouse's Work-Family Conflict, and Relationship Quality.* Bowling : Bowling Green State University.

Northcentral University Library. (2018, January 4). *Research Process*. Retrieved from Northcentral University Library: https://ncu.libguides.com/researchprocess

Novikova, I. (2013). Trait, Trait Theory. In K. D. Keith, *The Encyclopedia of Cross-Cultural Psychology.* John Wiley & Sons.

OCED. (2015). *How's Life in New Zealand.* OCED.

OECD. (2016). *OECD Better Life Index*. Retrieved from OECD: http://www.oecdbetterlifeindex.org/topics/work-life-balance/

OECD. (2017). *OECD Economic Surveys.* OECD.

OECD. (2018). *Labour Market Statistics .* Paris: OECD.

Ojo, S. I. (2012). *Work–Life Balance Policies and Practices in Nigeria: Experiences from Managerial and Non Managerial Employees in the Banking Sector.* London: Stella Ibiyinka Ojo.

Oláh, L. S., & Fahlén, S. (2013). Introduction: Aspirations and Uncertainties. Childbearing Choices and Work–Life Realities in Europe. In L. S. Oláh, & E. Fratczak, *Childbearing, Women's Employment and Work–Life Balance Policies in Contemporary Europe* (pp. 1-27). London: Palgrave Macmillan.

Oltmanns, T. F., & Turkheimer, E. (2009). Person Perception and Personality Pathology. *Current Directions in Psychological Science*, 32-36.

Oltmanns, T. F., & Turkheimer, E. (2009). Person Perception and Personality Pathology. *Curr Dir Psychol Sc*, 32-36.

Olund, V. L. (2016). *A Qualitative Study of Email Overload and Virtual Working Women's Self-Perceived Job-Related Stress and Work-Life Balance* . ProQuest LLC.

Orkibi, H., & Brandta, Y. I. (2015). HowPositivityLinksWithJobSatisfaction:PreliminaryFindingsonthe MediatingRoleofWork-LifeBalance. *Europe's Journal of Psychology, 11*(3), 406-418. doi:10.5964/ejop.v11i3.869

Ormel, J., Jerominus, B. F., Kotov, R., Riese, H., Bos, E. H., Hankin, B., . . . Oldehinkel, A. J. (2013). Neuroticism and commom mental disoders: Meaning and utility of a complex relationship. *Clinical Psychology Review*, 687-695.

Osborne, T. (1998). *Aspects of enlightenment.* London: UCL Press.

Oshio, A., Abe, S., & Cutrone, P. (2012). Development, Reliability, and Validity of the Japanese Version of Ten Item Personality Inventory (TIPI-J). *The Japanese Journal of Personality*, 21-40.

Oshio, A., Abe, S., Cutrone, P., & Gosling, S. D. (2014). Further validity of the Japanese version of the Ten Item Personality Inventory (TIPI-J): Cross-language evidence for content validity. *Journal of Individual Differences*, 236-244.

Otis, E. (2009). The Paradox of Flexibility: Guilt, Regret, and Work/Life Balance for Today's Mother. *Advances in Communication Theory & Research*, 2-35.

Otusile, E., Ibeh, J. M., & Ndubuisi, U. (2017). Finding Sustainable Balance Between Your Work And Personal Life. *International Journal of Innovative Research and Advanced Studies*, 328-332.

Owens, J., Kottwitz, C., Tiedt, J., & Ramirez, J. (2018). Strategies to Attain Faculty Work-Life BalancE. *Building Healthy Academic Communities Journal*, 58-73.

Oxford Brookes University. (2004). *Work-Life Balance: An audit of staff experience at Oxford Brookes University.* Wheatley: The Centre for Diversity Policy Research, Oxford Brookes University.

Padmanabhan, M., & Kumar, S. S. (2016). Work-Life Balance and Work-Life Conflict on Career Advancement of Women Professionals in Information and Communication Technology Sector, Bengaluru, India. *International Journal of Research*, 119-130. doi:10.5281/zenodo.56642

Padmasiri, M., & Mahalekamge, W. (2016). Impact of Demographical Factors on Work Life Balance among Academic Staff of University of Kelaniya, Sri Lanka. *Journal of Education and Vocational Research*, 54-59.

Pandu, A., Balu, A., & Poorani, K. (2013). Assessing Work-Life Balance among IT & ITeS Women Professional. *The Indian Journal of Industrial Relations*, 611-620.

Pandya, S. P., & Halsall, J. (2016). Aging spiritually: Pitamaha Sadans in India. In *Cogent Social Sciences.*

Parida, S. K. (2012, June). Measuring the Work Life Balance: An Inter-Personal study of the employees in IT and ITes Scctor. *An International Business Research Journal, 1*(1), 79-90. Retrieved from www.jbmcr.org

Paris, J. (2005). Borderline Personality Disoder . *CMAJ*, 1579-1583.

Parker, C. C., & Citera, M. (2010). Changing Roles: Are Millennials Redefining Work-Life Balance. Atlanta: Society for Industrial-Organizational Psychology.

Patel, S. P. (2009). *Work-Family Balance and Religion: A Resource Based Perspective.* The University of Tennessee. Chattanooga: Shivani P. Patel.

Patel, S. P., & Cunningham, C. J. (2012). Religion, resources, and work-family balance. *Mental Health, Religion & Culture*, 389-401. doi:10.1080/13674676.2011.577765

Patwa, P. (2011). Work Life Balance: A cross sectional study of Banking & Insurance Sector. *International Journal of Research in Commerce, IT & Management*, 85-91.

Pearson, E., & Podeschi, R. (1997). Humanism and individualism: Maslow and his critics. *Adult Education Research Conference.* Stillwater: New Prairie Press.

Peter Watson. (2017). *Imaging.mrc.* Retrieved from Effect Size: http://imaging.mrc-cbu.cam.ac.uk

Pfeffer, J. (1983). Organizational demography. *Research in Organizational Behavior*, 299-357.

Poelmans, S., Odle-Dusseau, H. N., & Beham, B. (2008). Work-life balance: Individual and organizational strategies and practices. In *The Oxford Handbook of Organizational Well Being* (pp. 180-213). Oxford University Press.

Possenriede, D., & Plantenga, J. (2003). Temporal and locational flexibility of work, working-time fit and job satisfaction. *Discussion Paper Series nr: 14-08* (pp. 2-32). Utrecht : Utrecht University.

Poulose, S., & Sudarsan, N. (2014). Work Life Balance: A Conceptual Review. *International Journal of Advances in Management and Economics, 3*(2), 1-17. Retrieved from www.managementjournal.info

Powell, G. N., & Greenhaus, J. H. (2006). THINK PIECE Is the opposite of positive negative? Untangling the complex relationship between work-family enrichment and conflict. *Career Development International, 11*(7), 650-659. doi:10.1108/13620430610713508

Prabhu, N. (2017, April 2017). Labour participation rate of women in India visibly low, says World Bank study. *The Hindu*.

Pradhan, R. K., Jena, L. K., & Kumari, I. G. (2016). Effect of Work-Life Balance on Organizational Citizenship Behaviour: Role of Organisational Commitment. *Global Business Review*, 1-15. doi:10.1177/0972150916631071

Prithi, S., & Vasumathi, A. (2018). The Influence of Demographic Profile on Work Life Balance of Women Employees in Tannery Industry – An Empirical Study. *Pertanika J. Soc. Sci. & Hum*, 259-284.

Pulvers, K., & Hood, A. (2013). The Role of Positive Traits and Pain Catastrophizing in Pain Perception. *Current Pain and Headache Reports*. doi:10.1007/s11916-013-0330-2

Raad, B. D. (2009). Structural models of personality. In *The Cambridge Handbook of Personality Psychology* (pp. 127-147). Cambridge: Cambridge University Press.

Raj, A. E., & Julius, S. (2015). Working Father and their Perceived Work – Life Balance with Special Reference to Hyundai Motors (I) Private Limited at Chennai. *International Journal of Advanced Scientific Research & Development*, 54-63.

Raj.R, A. (2013). A Study on Work-Life Balance of Employees in Pharma Marketing. *International Research Journal of Pharmacy*, 209-211.

Raj.R, A., & Ramanathan, H. N. (2012). A Study of Work-Life Balance of Paramedical Employees with Special Reference to a Private Hospital. *Indian Journal of Commerce & Management Studies*, 74-79.

Raja, S., & Stein, S. L. (2014). Work–Life Balance: History, Costs, and Budgeting for Balance. *Clinics in Colon and Rectal Surgery, 27*(2), 71-74.

Rajkumar, R. (2014). *Work Life Balance of IT Professionals in Relation to their Self Consept, Hardiness, and Emotional Maturity. .* PhD Thesis, Annamalai University, Department of Business Administration, Annamalai Nagar.

Raju, G. (2012). Work-Life Balancing Activities: Implications and Solutions. *International Journal of Social Science and Interdisciplinary Research*, 34-44.

Rania, S., Kamalanabhan, & Selvarania. (2011). Work-Life Balance Reflections on Employee Satisfaction. *Serbian Journal of Management*, 85-96.

Rantanen, J., Kinnunen, U., Mauno, S., & Tement, S. (2013). Patterns of conflict and enrichment in work-family balance: A three-dimensional typology. *An International Journal of Work, Health & Organisations , 27*(2), 141-163. doi:10.1080/02678373.2013.791074

Rantanen, J., Kinnunen, U., MaunO, S., & Tillemann, K. (2010). Introducing Theoretical Approaches to Work-Life Balance and Testing a New Typology Among Professionals. In S. Kaiser, M. J. Ringlstetter, D. R. Eikhof, & M. P. Cunha (Eds.), *Creating Balance?* (pp. 27-46). Springer Berlin Heidelberg. doi:10.1007/978-3-642-16199-5

Rantanen, J., Kinnunen, U., Mauno, S., & Tillemann, K. (2011). Introducing Theoretical Approaches to Work-Life Balance and Testing a New Typology Among Professionals. In S. Kaiser, M. Ringlstetter, D. Eikhof, & M. P. Cunha, *Creating Balance? International Prespectives on the Work-Life Integration of Professionals* (pp. 27-46). Berlin: Springer.

Rao, M. V. (2015). The influence of Personal and Demographic Factors on Work-Life Balance of Employees in Corporate Sector. *Pezzottaite Journals*, 1815-1822.

Rao, P. V. (2016). Work-Life Balance in Service Sector (Special Reference to Public and Private Sectors in Guntur Dist). *International Journal of Research and Development - A Management Review*, 69-75.

Ratna, R., Gupta, N., Devani, K., & Chawla, S. (2011, November). Work-Life Balance in BPO Sector. *International Journal of Physical and Social Science, 1*(3), 79-107. Retrieved from http://www.ijmra.us

Ravikumar, T. (2011). A Study on Work-Life Balance of BPO Employees in India. *International Journal of Research in IT, Management and Engineering*, 174-193.

Ray, S. (2018, January 28). *What is "Organized Religion"?* Retrieved from Catholicconvert.com: http://www.catholicconvert.com/blog/2018/01/28/what-does-the-nefarious-organized-religion-mean-to-many-protestants/

Raykov, T., & Marcoulides, G. A. (2006). *A First Course in Structural Equation Modeling.* Mahwah: Lawrence Erlbaum Associates, Inc.

Reddy, N. K., Vranda, M. N., Ahmed, A., Nirmala, B. P., & Siddaramu, B. (2010). Work–Life Balance among Married Women Employees. *Indian Journal of Psychological Medicine*, 112-118. doi:10.4103/0253-7176.78508

Redmond, J., Valiulis, M., & Drew, E. (2006). *Literature review of issues related to work-life balance, workplace culture and maternity/childcare issues.* Dublin: Crisis Pregnancy Agency.

Regoniel, P. A. (2015). *Two Tips on How to Write the Significance of the Study.* Retrieved from SimplyEducate.Me: http://simplyeducate.me

Rehman, S., & Roomi, M. A. (2012). Gender and work-life balance: a phenomenological study of Women entrepreneurs in Pakistan. *Journal of Small Business and Enterprise Development*, 209-228. doi:10.1108/14626001211223865

Reindl, C. U., Kaiser, S., & Stolz, M. L. (2011). Integrating Professional Work and Life: Conditions, Outcomes and Resources. In S. Kaiser, M. J. Ringlstetter,

D. R. Eikhof, & M. P. Cunha (Eds.), *Creating Balance?* (pp. 3-26). London: Springer. doi:10.1007/978-3-642-16199-5

Renaua, V., Obersta, U., Goslingb, S. D., Rusiñola, J., & Chamarroc, A. (2013). Translation and validation of the TenItem-Personality Inventory into Spanish and Catalan. *Revista de Psicologia*, 85-97.

Rendall, M. (2014). *The Service Sector and Female Market Work.* Zurich: University of Zurich.

Rennar, H. (2007). In search of true work/life balance: in order to consistently attain work/life balance, we must change our work ethic and corporate culture through education, acceptance, communication and accountability.(YOUR CAREER). *Financial Executive*. Retrieved from https://www.highbeam.com/doc/1G1-162875480.html

Renthlei, L., & Singh, A. K. (2015). Impact of Demographic Variables on Work-Life Balance of Teachers: A Study of Private Unaided Schools in Aizawl West Region of Mizoram in India. *Pezzottaite Journals*, 1920-1926.

Rice, R. W., Frone, M. R., & McFarlin, D. B. (1992). Work-nonwork conflict and the perceived quality of life. *Journal of Organizational Behavior*, 155-168.

Rieser, R. (2006). Disability equality: confronting the oppression of the past . In M. Cole, *Education, Equality and Human Rights* (pp. 134-156). Oxfordshire: Routledge.

Rincy, V., & Panchanatham, N. (2010). Development of A Psychometric Instrument to Measure Work-life Balance. *Continental J. Social Sciences*, 50-58.

Roberts, B. W., Jackson, J. J., Fayard, J. V., & Edmonds, G. (2013). Conscientiousness. In M. R. Leary, & R. H. Hoyle, *Handbook of Individual Differences in Social Behavior* (pp. 369-381). New York: Guilford Publications.

Robson, C., & Mccartan, K. (2016). *Real World Research A Resource for Users of Social Research Methods in Applied Settings.* London: John Wiley & Sons Ltd.

Rosic, A. (2017). *What is Cryptocurrency: Everything You Need To Know [Ultimate Guide].* Retrieved from https://blockgeeks.com/guides/what-is-cryptocurrency/

Rosseel, Y. (2012). lavaan: An R Package for Structural Equation . *Journal of Statistical Software*, 1-36.

Rosta, G. (2012). Religiosity and Political Values in Central and Eastern Europe. In G. Pickel, & K. Sammet, *Transformations of Religiosity Religion and Religiosity in Eastern Europe 1989 – 2010* (pp. 95-110). Wiesbaden: Springer VS.

Rothberg, S. (2014). *The Journey of Female Cancer Patients or Survivors while Striving for Personal Work-life Balance .* ProQuest LLC.

Ruderman, M., Ohlott, P., Panzer, K., & King, S. N. (2002). Benefits of Multiple Roles for Managerial Women. *The Academy of Management Journal*, 369-386.

Russo, M., Shteigman, A., & Carmeli, A. (2015). Workplace and family support and work–life balance: Implications for individual psychological availability and energy at work. *The Journal of Positive Psychology*, 173-188. doi:10.1080/17439760.2015.1025424

Rutland, A. (2004). *Doing Social Psychology Research.* (G. M. Breakwell, Ed.) Main Street, Malden, MA 02148-5020, USA: The British Psychological Society and Blackwell Publishing Ltd.

Sakthivel, D., & Jayakrishnan, J. (2010). Work life balance and Organizational commitment for Nurses. *Asian Journal of Business and Management Sciences, 2*(5), 1-6.

Saltzstein, A. L., Ting, Y., & Saltzstein, G. H. (2001). Work-Family Balance and Job Satisfaction: The Impact of Family-Friendly Policies on Attitudes of Federal Government Employees. *Public Administration Review*, 452-467. doi:10.1111/0033-3352.00049

Sarkar, J. G., & Sarkar, A. (2017). Brand religiosity: An epistemological analysis of the formation of social anti-structure through the development of distinct brand sub-culture. *Society and Business Review*, 20-32.

Saucier, G. (2009). What Are the Most Important Dimensions of Personality?Evidence from Studies of Descriptors in Diverse Languages. *Social and Personality Psychology Compass*, 620-637.

Sav, A. (2016). The role of religion in work-life interface. *The International Journal of Human Resource Management*. doi:10.1080/09585192.2016.1255905

Sayer, A. (2010). *Realism and Social Science.* Delhi: Sage.

Schulz, U., & Schwarzer, R. (2003). Social support in coping with illness: The Berlin Social Support Scales. *Diagnostica*, 73-82.

Schwingshackl, A. (2014). The Fallacy of Chasing after Work-Life Balance. In J. H. Lee, *Frontiers in Pediatrics* (pp. 1-3). Frontiers.

Scott, A. B. (2011). Labour market flexibility and worker security in an age of migration. In M. Bommes, & G. Sciortino, *Foggy Social Structures Irregular Migration, European Labour Markets and the Welfare State* (pp. 143-168). Amsterdam: Amsterdam University Press.

Shaffert, R. (2011, May 25). *Workplace Flexibility and People with Disabilities.* Retrieved from Huffpost: https://www.huffingtonpost.com/robin-shaffert/workplace-flexibility-and_b_336852.html

Shagvaliyeva, S., & Yazdanifard, R. (2014). Impact of Flexible Working Hours on Work-Life Balance. *American Journal of Industrial and Business Management, 4*(1), 20-23. doi:10.4236/ajibm.2014.41004

Shah, S. S. (2014). *The Role of Work-Family Enrichment in WorkLife Balance & Career Success: A Comparison of German & Indian Managers.* Munich: Shalaka Sharad Shah.

Shah, S. S. (2014). *The Role of Work-Family Enrichment in WorkLife Balance & Career Success: A Comparison of German & Indian Managers.* Munich: Shalaka Sharad Shah.

Shahisaman, L. (2015). *A Phenomenological Study of Women in India Striving to Achieve Work-Life Balance in Finance with Competing Priorities.* Ann Arbor: ProQuest.

Shanafelt, T. D., Boone, S., Tan, L., Dyrbye, L. N., Sotile, W., Satele, D., . . . Oreskovich, M. R. (2012). Burnout and Satisfaction With Work-Life

Balance Among US Physicians Relative to the General US Population. *Arch Inters Med*, 501-509.

Shanafelt, T. D., Boone, S., Tan, L., Dyrbye, L. N., Sotile, W., Satele, D., . . . Oreskovich, M. R. (2012). Burnout and Satisfaction With Work-Life Balance Among US Physicians Relative to the General US Population. *Arch Intern Med*, 1377-1385. doi:10.1001/archinternmed.2012.3199

Sharma, B., & Nair, M. (2015). Work-Life Balance among Working Women in Service Sectors: A Conceptual Framework. *Pezzottaite Journals*, 1912-1917.

Sharma, J. K., & Mehta, D. (2009). A Study on Impact of Work-Life Balance Issues on Performance of Pharma Sales Managers.

Sharman, J. (2017, December 5). *Four Phases of Industrial Revolution: Phase One.* Retrieved from Thenbs: https://www.thenbs.com/knowledge/four-phases-of-industrial-revolution-phase-one

Shein, J., & Chen, C. P. (2011). *Work-Family Enrichment A Research of Positive Transfer.* Rotterdam: Sense Publishers.

Sheokand, K. S., & Priyanka. (2013). Work Life Balance: An Overview of Indian Companies. *International Journal of Research in Commerce and Management*, 138-143.

Shiva, G. (2013). A Study on Work Family Balance and Challenges Faced By Working Women. *IOSR Journal of Business and Management, 14*(5), 1-4. Retrieved from www.iosrjournals.org

Shukla, A., & Srivastava, R. (2016). Development of short questionnaire to measure an extended set of role expectation conflict, coworker support and work-life balance: The new job stress scale. *Cogent Business & Management*, 2-19. doi:10.1080/23311975.2015.1134034

Shylaja, P., & Prasad, C. (2017). Emotional Intelligence and Work Life Balance. *Journal of Business and Management*, 18-21.

Simonea, S. D., Agusa, M., Lasioa, D., & Serria, F. (2018). Development and Validation of a Measure of Work-Family Interface. *Journal of Work and Organizational Psychology*. doi:10.5093/jwop2018a19

Singh, G. (2018, Febuary 25). Fewer job hours can improve work-life balance. *Indian Express*.

Singh, S. (2013). Work - Life Balance: A Literature Review. *Global Journal of Commerce & Management Perspective, 2*(3), 84-91.

Singh, S. (2014). Mesuring Work-life Balance in India. *International Journal of Advance Research in Computer Science and Management Studies, 2*(5), 35-43. Retrieved from www.ijarcms.com

Sinha, D. (2014). Study of Work Life Balance @ CCIL (India), NOIDA. *Journal of Management Sciences And Technology*, 8-14.

Smeltzer, S. C., Cantrell, M. A., Sharts-Hopko, N. C., Heverly, M. A., Jenkinson, A., & Nthenge, S. (2016, April). Psychometric Analysis of the Work/Life Balance Self-Assessment Scale. *Journal of Nursing Measurement, 24*(1), 5-14. doi:10.1891/1061-3749.24.1.5

Smith, J., & Gardner, D. (2007). Factors Affecting Employee Use of Work-Life Balance Initiatives. *New Zealand Journal of Psychology, 32*(1), 3-12.

Smithson, J., & Stokoe, E. H. (2005). Discourses of Work–Life Balance: Negotiating 'Genderblind' Terms in Organizations. In *Gender, Work and Organization* (pp. 147-168). Malden: Blackwell Publishing Ltd.

Staines, G. L. (1980). Spillover Versus Compensation: A Review of the Literature on the Relationship Between Work and Nonwork. *Human Relations, 33*(2), 111-129. doi:10.1177/001872678003300203

Staines, G. L., & O'Connor, P. (1980). Conflicts among Work, Leisure, and Family Roles. *Monthly Labor Review, 103*(8), 35-39. Retrieved from http://www.jstor.org/stable/41841305

St-Amour, N., Laverdure, J., Devault, A., & Manseau, S. (2007). *The Difficulty of Balancing Work and Family Life: Impact on the Physical and Mental Health of Quebec Families.* Institut national de santé publique du Québec.

State Services Commission New Zealand . (2005). *Work-Life Balance: a resource for the State Services.* State Services Commission New Zealand: Wellington .

Stephens, G. K., & Sommer, S. M. (1996). The Measurement of Work to Family Conflict. *Educational and Psychological Measurement*, 475-486. doi:10.1177/0013164496056003009

Sturges, J., & Guest, D. (2004). Working to live or living to work? Work/life balance early in the career. *Human Resource Management Journal, 14*(4), 5-20.

Sudha.D, Anitha.S, & Harikumar, P. (2016). Impact of Job Related issues on the Work-Life Balance of Women. *International Journal of Advanced Research in ISSN: 2278-6236 Management and Social Sciences*, 311-329.

Sundaresan, S. (2014). Work-Life Balance-Implication for Working Women. *International Journal of Sustainable Development*, 93-102. Retrieved from http://www.ssrn.com/link/OIDA-Intl-Journal-Sustainable-Dev.html

Suresh, S., & Kodikal, R. (2017). SEM approach to explore Work Life Balance: A study among nurses of Multispecialty Hospitals. *Sahyadri Journal of Management*, 1-16.

Swarnalatha, C., & Rajalakshmi, S. (2015). Examining the Role Of Organization In Providing Healthy Work Life Balance And Its Impact On Psychological Outcomes. In *International Conference on Inter Disciplinary Research in Engineering and Technology* (pp. 214-221). Retrieved from www.icidret.in

Szener, J. B., Grzankowski, K. S., Eng, K. H., Odunsi, K., & Frederick, P. J. (2016). Evaluation of satisfaction with work-life balance among U.S Gynecologic Oncology Fellows: A cross-sectional study. *Gynecologic Oncology Reports*, 17-20. Retrieved from http://dx.doi.org/10.1016/j.gore.2016.03.001

Szmaragd, C., & Leckie, G. (2011). Module 5: Introduction to Multilevel Modelling . In C. Szmaragd, & G. Leckie, *Multilevel Modelling.* Centre for Multilevel Modelling.

Tabachnick, B. G., & Fidell, L. S. (2013). *Using Multivariate Statistics.* Boston: Pearson.

Takács, J. (2013). Unattainable Desires? Childbearing Capabilities in Early 21st-Century Hungary. In L. S. Oláh, & E. Fra̧tczak, *Childbearing, Women's*

Employment and Work–Life Balance Policies in Contemporary Europe (pp. 179-206). New York: Palgrave Macmillan.

Takashima, I. (2010). *Bitcoin: The Ultimate Guide to the World of Bitcoin, Bitcoin Mining, Bitcoin Investing, Blockchain Technology, Cryptocurrency.* Kindle Edition.

Talukder, A. H. (2011). A Shifting Paradigm of Work-Life Balance in Service Context-An Empirical Study . *Indus Journal of Management & Social Sciences*, 10-23.

Tambe, S. (2017). Work-life Balance and Gender Bias : A Contrarian View. *International Journal of Business and Management*, 14-16.

Tamsett, J. (2015). The Ultimate Guide to Work/Life Balance. *Optimum Health Magazine* . Analee Matthews.

Tariq, A., Aslam, H. D., Siddique, A., & Tanveer, A. (2012). Work-Life Balance as a Best Practice Model of Human Resource Management: A Win-Win Situational Tool for the Employees and Organizations. *Mediterranean Journal of Social Sciences, 3*(1), 577-585. doi:10.5901/mjss.2012.03.01.577

Tausig, M., & Fenwick, R. (2001). Unbinding Time: Alternate Work Schedules and Work-Life Balance. *Journal of Family and Economic Issues, 22*(2), 101-119.

Taylor, R. (2010). The Future of Work-Life Balance. *An ESRC Future of Work Programme Seminar Serie* (pp. 1-21). Swindon: E.E.R.C Economic and Social Research Council.

Team, G. (2017). *Top 20 Employee Benefits & Perks for 2017.* Retrieved from glassdoor: https://www.glassdoor.com/blog/top-20-employee-benefits-perks-for-2017/

Thakur, S., & Surampudi, S. (2011). Attaining Work – Life Balance : Strategies For Increasing Work Productivity. *VSRD International Journal of Business & Management Research, 1*(2), 115-120. Retrieved from www.visualsoftindia.com/journal.html

The Economic Times. (2017, January 10). Tax notices slapped on cryptocurrency investors as trading hits $3.5 billion. Retrieved from https://economictimes.indiatimes.com/topic/cryptocurrency

The Original Information Culture – Ice Age Hunter/Gatherers. (2012, May 14). Retrieved January 17, 2016, from Hunter/Gatherers to Digital Natives: Six Information Revolutions: http://information-revolutions.com

The Writer's Handbook. (2016, November 3). Retrieved from The Writing Center @ University of Wisconsin - Madison: http://www.writing.wisc.edu/

The Writing Center, University of North Carolina at Chapel Hill. (2014). Retrieved from The University of North Carolina at Chapel Hill: http://www.unc.edu/

Thomas, L. T., & Ganster, D. C. (1995). Impact of Family-Supportive Work Variables on Work-Family Conflict and Strain: A Control Perspective. *Journal of Applied Psychology, 80*(1), 6-15.

Thompson, C. (2006). *Under Pressure: Implication of Work-Family Conflict and Job Stress.* Toronto: Human Solutions.

Thyer, B. A. (2008). The Importance of Journal Articles. In B. A. Thyer, *Preparing Research Articles* (pp. 20-43). New York: Oxford University Press. doi:DOI:10.1093/acprof:oso/9780195323375.003.0001

Tiedje, L. B., Downey, g., & Wortman, C. (1990). Women with Multiple Roles: Role-Compatibility Perceptions, Satisfaction, and Mental Health. *Journal of Marriage and the Family*, 63-72.

Timmis, C., Brough, P., Siu, O. L., O'Driscoll, M., & Kalliath, T. (2015). Handbook of research on work-life balance in Asia. In *Cross-cultural impact of work-life balance on health and work outcomes* (pp. 294-314).

Tingley, D., Yamamoto, T., Hirose, K., Keele, L., & Imai, K. (2017, July 12). Causal Mediation Analysis . *Package'mediation'.*

Toffoletti, K., & Starr, K. (2016). Women Academics and Work–Life Balance: Gendered Discourses of Work and Care. *Gender, Work & Organization*, 6-20. doi:doi:10.1111/gwao.12133

Torgersen, S., & Vollrath, M. E. (2006). Personality Types, Personality Traits, and Risky Health Behavior. In M. E. Vollrath, *Handbook of Personality and*

Health (pp. 215-234). The Atrium, Southern Gate, Chichester, West Sussex : John Wiley & Sons Ltd,.

Toston, S. (2014). *Work-life Balance Straegies of Women Leaders within the Church of God in Christ.* Ann Arbor: ProQuest LLC.

Trindade, H. (2016). *How to Manage Stress with Self-Awareness.* (G. Bichard, Ed.) Hilton Trindade.

Triplett, J. (2016). *The Work-Life Balance of Female Adjunct Faculty at Southern California Community Colleges.* Ann Arbor: ProQuest LLC.

Tsao, W.-C., & Chang, H.-R. (2010). Exploring the impact of personality traits on online shopping behavior. *African Journal of Business Management*, 1801-1812.

Tsui, A. S., & O'Reilly, C. A. (1989). Beyond Simple Demographic Effects: The Importance of Relational Demography in Superior-Subordinate Dyads. *The Academy of Management Journal*, 402-423.

Tuğsal, T. (2017). The Effects of Socio-Demographic Factors and Work-Life Balance on Employees' Emotional Exhaustion. *Journal of Human Science*, 654-665.

Ufoegbune, V. I. (2016). *A Phenomenological Study of the Work–life balance of Nigerian Women Leadership and their vision of Nigerian Education .* Ph.D Thesis.

UK Essays. (2013, November). *The Concept Of Work Life Balance.* Retrieved from UKESSAYS: https://www.ukessays.com/essays/social-work/the-concept-of-work-life-balance-social-work-essay.php

Umene-Nakano, W., Kato, T. A., Kikuchi, S., Tateno, M., Fujisawa, D., Hoshuyama, T., & Nakamura, J. (2013). Nationwide Survey of Work Environment, Work-Life Balance and Burnout among Psychiatrists in Japan. *Plos One, 8*(2), 1-8.

University of Cambridge. (2017, December 12). *Rules of thumb on magnitudes of effect sizes.* Retrieved from University of Cambridge: http://imaging.mrc-cbu.cam.ac.uk/statswiki/FAQ/effectSize

University of Cambridge. (2018, June 14). *Rules of thumb on magnitudes of effect sizes.* Retrieved from MRC Cognition and Brain Science Unit: http://imaging.mrc-cbu.cam.ac.uk/statswiki/FAQ/effectSize

Valcour, M. (2007). Work-Based Resources as Moderators of the Relationship Between Work Hours and Satisfaction With Work-Family Balance. *Journal of Applied Psychology, 92*(6), 1512-1523. doi:10.1037/0021-9010.92.6.1512

Valk, R., & Srinivasan, V. (2011). Work-family Balance of Indian women software professionals: A qualitative study. *IIMB Management Review*, 40-50.

Vanishree. (2012, November). Work-life Balance in the BPO Sector. *Journal of Business Management and Social Science Research, 1*(2), 35-39. Retrieved from www.borjournals.com

Vijayalakshmi, B., & Latha, G. (2013). Work Life Balance: A Study on University Faculty of Sri Padmavathi Mahila Visvavidyalam, Tirupathi. *International Journal of Commerce, Economics and Management, 3*(4), 37-41. Retrieved from http://ijrcm.org.in/

Villiers, J. D., & Kotze, E. (2003). Work-Life Balance A study in Petroleum Industry. *Journal of Human Resource Management*, 15-23.

Visser, F., & Williams, L. (2006). *Work-Life Balance: Rhetoric Versus Reality.* London: The Work Foundation.

Viswanathan, K., & Jeyakumaran. (2013, Auguest). Instrument Development for Studying Work Life Balance Programs in Information Technology Firms. *Journal of Business and Management, 11*(4), 47-53. Retrieved from www.iosrjournals.org

Vlems, E. (2005). *Work-Life Balance.* Geel: Katholieke Hogeschool Kempen.

Voydanoff, P. (2005). Toward a Conceptualization of Perceived Work-Family Fit and Balance: A Demands and Resources Approach. *Journal of Marriage and Family*, 822-836.

Walliman, N. (2011). *Research Methods the basics.* New York: Routledge.

Waumsley, J. A., Houston, D. M., & Marks, G. (2010). What about Us? Measuring the Work-Life Balance of People Who Do Not Have Children. *Review of European Studies*, 3-17.

Wayne, J. H., Grzywacz, J. G., Carlson, D., & Kacmar, M. (2007). Work-family facilitation: A theoretical explanation and model of primary antecedents and consequences. *Human Resource Management Review*, 63-76. doi:10.1016/j.hrmr.2007.01.002

Wayne, J. H., Musisca, N., & Fleeson, W. (2004). Considering the role of personality in the work-family experience: Relationships of the Big Five to work-family conflict and facilitation. *Journal of Vocational Behavior*, 108-130. doi:10.1016/S0001-8791(03)00035-6

Weegar, M. A., & Pacis, D. (2012). A Comparison of Two Theories of Learning - Behaviorism and Constructivism as applied to Face-to-Face and Online Learning. *E-Leader Manila* , 2012.

Weinstein, S. M. (2009). Workplace Balance. In S. M. Weinstein, *B is for balance : a nurse's guide for enjoying life at work and at home* (pp. 67-80). Renee Wilmeth .

Wepfer, A. G., Brauchli, R., Gregor J. Jenny, O. H., & Bauer, G. F. (2015). The experience of work-life balance across family-life stages in Switzerland: a cross-sectional questionnaire-based study. *BMC Public Health*, 1-11. doi:10.1186/s12889-015-2584-6

White, M., Hill, S., McGovern, P., Mills, C., & Smeaton, D. (2003). 'High-performance' Management Practices, Working Hours and Work–Life Balance. *British Journal of Industrial Relations*, 175-195.

Whitehead, D. (2013). Searching and reviewing the research literature. In *Nursing & Midwifery Research: Methods and Appraisal for Evidence-Based Practice* (pp. 35-56).

Widiger, T. A., Gore, W. L., Crego, C., Rojas, S. L., & Oltmanns, J. R. (2016). Five-Factor Model and Personality Disorder. In T. A. Widiger, *The Oxford Handbook of the Five Factor Model of Personality* (pp. 1-62). Oxford: Oxford University Press.

Wilt, J., & Revelle, W. (2013). Extraversion. In M. R. Leary, & R. H. Hoyle, *Handbook of Individual Differences in Social Behavior* (pp. 27-45). New York: Guilford Publications.

Winchester, C. L., & Salji, M. (2016). Writing a Literature Review. *Journal of Clinical Urology*, 308-312.

Wittenberg-Cox, A. (2018, February 26). *Being a Two-Career Couple Requires a Long-Term Plan.* Retrieved from Harvard Business Review: https://hbr.org/2018/02/being-a-two-career-couple-requires-a-long-term-plan

WLB & D. (2018, April 24). *Living with a Disability*. Retrieved from Work-Life Balance and Disability: http://work-life-disability.org/#wlbd

Write a Literature Review. (2016, October 25). Retrieved from University of California: http://guides.library.ucsc.edu/write-a-literature-review

Write Like a Scientist. (2017, April 19). *Gap Statements*. Retrieved from Write Like a Scientist: http://sites.middlebury.edu/middsciwriting/overview/organization/gap-statements/

Wu, A. H. (2017). *Work-Life Balance: A Study of Personality Factors as a Predictor of Work-Life Boundary Permability and Use of Enterprise Social Media and Technology.* East Carolina University. East Carolina: Allison H Wu.

Wua, L., Rusyidib, B., Claibornec, N., & McCarthy, M. L. (2013). Relationships between work–life balance and job-related factors among child welfare workers. *Children and Youth Services Review*, 1447-1454. Retrieved from https://doi.org/10.1016/j.childyouth.2013.05.017

Yadav, R. K., & Dabhade, N. (2013). Work life balance amongst the working women in public sector banks – a case study of State Bank of India. *International Letters of Social and Humanistic Sciences*, 1-22.

Yawalkar, V. V., & Sonawane, M. A. (2017). Impact of Demographic Variables on Work-Life Balance of Police Personnel: With Reference To Jalgaon Police Department. *International Journal of Science, Engineering and Management*, 29-32.

Yuile, C., Chang, A., & Gudmundsson, A. (2005). Life friendly policies:Do they really help? In Fisher, & R. Huges, *Engaging the Multiple Contexts of Management: Convergence and Divergence of Management Theory and Practice: Proceedings of the 19th ANZAM Conference* (pp. 1-12). Canaberra: Queensland University of Technology.

Zakaria, A., & Omar, M. K. (2016). Manifestation of work-life balance in the Malaysian banking workforce: Transformational leadership the potent enabler. *7thAsia-Pacific International Conference on Environment-Behaviour Studies*, 279-287. Retrieved from www.e-iph.co.uk

Zakaria, M. F., Mat, N., & Abdullah, A. R. (2018). Pengaruh Personaliti Big Five Kepada Keseimbangan Kerja-Kehidupan: Perspektif Guru. *International Journal of Education, Psychology and Counseling*, 21-31.

Zarzycka, B. (2008). Religiosity in Poland Tradition or Charisma — Religiosity in Poland . In L. Mohn, *Religion Monitor 2008 | EUROPE Overview of religious attitudes and practices* (pp. 26-29). Religion Monitor.

Zhang, H., Yip, P. S., Chi, P., Chan, K., Cheung, Y. T., & Zhang, X. (2012). Factor Structure and Psychometric Properties of the Work-Family Balance Scale in an Urban Chinese Sample. *Soc Indic Res*, 409-418. doi:10.1007/s11205-010-9776-3

Zheng, C., Kashi, K., Fan, D., Molineux, o., & Ee, M. S. (2015). Impact of individual coping strategies and organisational work–life balance programmes on Australian employee well-being. *The International Journal of Human Resource Management*, 501-526. doi:10.1080/09585192.2015.1020447

Zocket. (2017, June). *How Does Your Personality Compare?* Retrieved from Zocket: https://zocket.me